Conquering Depression

Conquering Depression

A 30-Day Plan to Finding Happiness

Mark A. Sutton & Bruce Hennigan, M.D.

BROADMAN
& HOLMAN
PUBLISHERS

Nashville, Tennessee

Published by Broadman & Holman Publishers,
Nashville, Tennessee

ISBN 0-7394-1680-4

Mark dedicates this book to:
My wife, Susan,
who has made my life far richer
than I could ever have imagined.

Bruce dedicates this book to:
My wife, Sherry,
whose patient love led me
out of the darkness.

CONTENTS

Part 3: Three Key Medicines for the Body and Soul / 79

Part 4: Small Weapons That Win a Big Victory / 101

Part 5: The Exit Signs That Lead You Out of Depression / 135

Part 6: Three Attitude-Affirmers That Stop Depression from Starting / 169

PREFACE

[Mark] Several years ago, I made an offhand comment during a Sunday morning sermon that changed both my ministry and the lives of many people. The statement went something like this: "God has taught me much over the years as I've struggled with overcoming depression." Both immediately after the service and all through the following weeks, person after person came up to me and thanked me for my "bravery" in admitting I fought depression on a regular basis. I hadn't thought of it as being brave. I had simply wanted to share with other believers how God was working in my life on a daily basis to give me the spiritual and emotional strength I needed.

Nonetheless, many hurting individuals appreciated what they saw as a refreshing candor. They began coming to my office and asking for help in dealing with this pernicious, much misunderstood disease. And they all had the same question: Why has the Christian community been so silent about addressing depression?

As I shared with both individuals and groups practical, biblical advice on how to deal with depression, God began freeing Christians. Hurting men and women finally found victory over an aspect of their lives they'd been ashamed to admit existed. Their stories, in turn, encouraged others to discover the freedom of victory in their emotional life.

One of those who truly overcame his depression was a young physician, Bruce Hennigan. Bruce had developed a system of daily reminders that literally transformed his life, strengthened his decision-making ability, and gave him control over his emotional outlook—but I'll let him tell you about it in his own words . . . .

[Bruce] I recall being amazed that my pastor and friend, Mark Sutton, suffered with recurrent bouts of depression. When I learned that he had gained victory over those horrible feelings of hopelessness, it gave me hope. For I had also undergone a long period of depression necessitating professional counseling. During that period, God led me to develop a series of tools designed to help overcome these negative emotions. Once Mark revealed his own personal struggle with depression, I found a sympathetic ear. I shared the details of my battle, including my most effective tool, the LifeFilter. Intrigued by our common experience, Mark asked me to help him write a book about depression, using both my personal experience and my medical knowledge. His vision was to share a simple, day-by-day program for understanding and overcoming depression with clear explanations of the medical aspects of the disease and solid biblical principles.

Just where did the concept of LifeFilters come from? Since the age of seventeen I have suffered from high blood pressure. Even though I was a teenager, I still required daily doses of medication. During the early months of my struggle with the worst depression of my life, I realized I could only overcome the disease with daily doses of mental "medication." What form would this preventive medication take?

I realized the process of depression involved the realm of the mind. Knowledge is the most powerful tool in overcoming the lies that the depressed mind conjures. One phrase I recalled from my counseling was, "What is the lie?" What falsehood had I bought into that made me so depressed? If I could ask myself that question every time I felt depressed, perhaps I could seek the answer—the knowledge that would lead me out of the darkness. Choosing the Word of God, I designed a simple card with a series of thought-provoking questions on one side and a scriptural answer on the other. I would choose a different card every day, and when I felt the wearying weight of depression fold its dark wings about me, I would take out the card and ask the questions. After identifying the "lie," I could then turn my attention to the truth of God's Word. Thus, the LifeFilter was born: a process of filtering my thoughts and emotions through a series of questions until the lies were removed and only the truth remained. The truth of God's Word. God's promise. God's knowledge. God's healing.

Final thoughts: This book, as you can see, is an explanation of what we've personally experienced. God has shown us, through his Word, how we can have victory over depression. And we want you to have this same victory. If you, or if someone you love, suffers from depression, this book is for you.

A pastor/counselor, a Christian physician, and the Bible: we've put together this team to lead you out of the shadows of depression and into the light of a healthy Christian life. As you'll see, we've already been praying for *you*. We welcome you as a part of our team. Together, with God's wisdom and strength, we can overcome depression and begin living the life God has designed for his children.

Part 1

*Building Your
Depression-Fighting Team*

DAY I
Finding Someone Who Understands

THE POWER TO WIN
Do any of these emotions describe you?
- Regularly depressed.
- Unable to grasp happiness.
- Lacking the energy to face the day.
- Experiencing guilt that threatens to overwhelm you.
- Deeply desiring a more fulfilling life.

Whatever your problem, *we want to give you immediate help*. In a moment, we'll explain how the book works. You'll receive some great tools and a lot of encouragement in the days to come. But if you are currently struggling with depression—or any other difficult emotion—you need something to help you right now!

So let us begin with this: *We understand!*

Both Dr. Hennigan and I have struggled with depression in the past (as well as most of the other emotions described in the opening paragraph), and we'll probably continue to fight such feelings in the future.

If you're depressed, you may feel alone and misunderstood. Perhaps friends or family members have told you to "cheer up," "think positive," or "quit feeling so sorry for yourself." By their comments, you know they do not understand the depth or seriousness of your problem.

We understand!

Depression can often leave you feeling guilty about anything and everything. It can cause you to doubt God's love for you. It can even make you wish life would end.

We understand!

That's why we are writing this book for you. We not only know what you're going through, *we've also discovered some powerful tools that can help you win the battle over depression . . . forever!*

One of the greatest helps we have is the wisdom found in God's Word. Take a moment to read the Scriptures below. We'll talk about them later in the week, but right now, just think about what they say to you. "Humble yourselves, therefore, under God's mighty hand, that he may lift you up in due time. *Cast all your anxiety on him because he cares for you*" (1 Pet. 5:6–7, italics added).

God loves you! And you can give him your anxieties because he cares! As you progress through this book, you'll discover how to experience this love and care in your own life.

Now let's take a look at the makeup of this book.

First, it is divided into thirty chapters, or "days." We have used this term for a reason: though you might enjoy doing so, the book is not designed to be read in one or two sittings. Instead, *Conquering Depression: A Thirty-Day Plan to Finding Happiness* should be read one day at a time. These bite-size chunks won't take long to absorb, are easy to digest, and should improve your spiritual and emotional health when taken on a daily basis.

Each day is divided into three sections: "The Power to Win"—positive steps you can take to ensure change in your emotional and physical well-being, coupled with Scriptures designed by God to help you ultimately triumph; "Strength for Today"—breakthroughs in medicine to help you conquer depression, guilt, and anger, analyzed and described from a Christian physician's perspective; and "Tools for Tomorrow"—LifeFilters that lead you, step-by-step, to help you analyze, understand, and solve your problems. Finally, a summary will help you wrap up and remember what you've just read.

For the next thirty days, we are going to be a team. In other words, you are not alone in fighting against depression. But Dr. Hennigan

(Bruce) and I want your team to extend far beyond this initial month. So we are going to help you put together a strong team that can stay with you for the rest of your life.

Alone, fighting depression is almost impossible. With a talented, caring team you can actually win the battle. In opening this book and reading this far, *you've already started winning*. Now let's finish what we've started!

STRENGTH FOR TODAY
Knowledge Is Power

In the early days of modern medicine, doctors were perplexed at the alarming number of patients who died following surgery. Men and women undergoing the simplest of operations died from an unknown, overwhelming process. Surgeons would operate without gloves or sterile technique and walk from one operation to another, unknowingly transmitting infection.

The problem? These surgeons did not know about the microscopic world of germs. Unwittingly, they transmitted death from one patient to another.

After the development of the microscope, these unseen harbingers of death became understood. Armed with the knowledge of the microscopic world, physicians finally comprehended the underlying problems, and the adoption of sterile techniques represented a major step forward in modern medicine. *Knowledge is power.*

> ## Tools for Tomorrow
>
> ### LIFEFILTER 1
>
> *How to Develop a Battle Plan*
> "If God is for us, who can be against us? He who did not spare his own Son, but gave him up for us all—how will he not also, along with him, graciously give us all things?" (Rom. 8:31b–32).
>
> #### TODAY
> 1. God loves me. And that's why I can win the battle against depression, because I've got God on my side.
> 2. Remember: God is greater than my depression.
> 3. Believe: God loves me, regardless of my emotional outlook!

Through knowledge, the physicians were able to understand the underlying cause of these horrible deaths. My goal as a physician is to help you understand the disease of depression. I will do this by helping you gain knowledge in the coming days concerning your body's and mind's relationship to the processes that bring about clinical depression. Through the process of education, you will become empowered with knowledge to combat depression.

Part of our effort to help you with depression will involve the use of LifeFilters.

In medicine, filters are used to screen out unwanted microscopic lifeforms in order to purify water. Without the filters the water might look pure, but it could contain deadly bacteria.

LifeFilters serve a similar purpose, helping you to screen out harmful thinking patterns leading to depression. Without the LifeFilters, your life might look good on the outside, but it could harbor negative, self-destructive habits.

Each day you will use a small card on which is printed a LifeFilter, a concept covered in The Power to Win and Strength for Today. On the flip side will be a Bible verse. By rooting yourself in the Word of God, you will begin empowering yourself spiritually to deal with that day. Think of the verse as a dose of antibiotic helping you to ward off the infection of depression.

LifeFilters are a tool. They remind you, gently, of what you have learned that day. Remember, learning leads to knowledge, and knowledge leads to understanding. Understanding depression empowers you to defeat it.

God's Word, LifeFilters, a Christian physician, and a Christian counselor: this is your team for the next thirty days. Together, we're going to help you learn to live above your depression!

SUMMARY

You're not alone in your depression. *We understand!* And the news gets even better. Read again 1 Peter 5:7. Did you know that God wrote that verse just for you? That's right! God loves you. He cares for you. And that's why you can win the battle against depression, because you've got God on your side.

And he understands!

Even if you have difficulty believing God loves you, take a moment to begin stretching your faith. We want you to pray and thank God for his love and care. If you need help, you can use the following prayer as a guideline:

> Dear Father, I want to thank you for your love and compassion. You know how I struggle with my emotions. Sometimes they get the best of me. In the middle of those difficult times, please help me remember that _you are greater than my depression._ Help me learn to trust in you no matter what my emotional outlook. And may this book be used by you to help me become stronger emotionally and spiritually. I ask these things in Jesus' name. Amen.

We look forward to seeing you tomorrow for day 2!

PHYSICIAN'S FACT

We want to help you understand the medical basis for depression. Learning about depression will empower you to conquer and defeat it.

DAY 2
Finding the Peace You Want

THE POWER TO WIN

Have you ever just wanted to give up and die? Have you ever prayed and asked God to take you out of this world so that you could escape your emotional or physical pain?

I have.

I've also counseled many others who felt the same way. As a matter of fact, one of the greatest men in the Bible, a powerful prophet who did many wonderful things for God, got discouraged and was ready to be taken out of this world.

Read his story:

> Elijah was afraid and ran for his life. When he came to Beersheba in Judah, he left his servant there, while he himself went a day's journey into the desert. He came to a broom tree, sat down under it and prayed that he might die. "I have had enough, LORD," he said. "Take my life; I am no better than my ancestors." . . .
>
> And the word of the LORD came to him: "What are you doing here, Elijah?"
>
> He replied, "I have been very zealous for the LORD God Almighty. The Israelites have rejected your covenant, broken down your altars, and put your prophets to death with the sword. I am the only one left, and now they are trying to kill me too." (1 Kings 19:3–4, 9b–10)

God answered every other prayer of Elijah's that is recorded. But God didn't answer this prayer!

Why?

- Elijah had his eyes on the difficulties of his circumstances. He should have kept his eyes on God.

> Elijah's emotions had so narrowed his focus that he could no longer see beyond himself.

- The prophet let his emotions interpret the seriousness of the situation. Instead, he should have let God intervene and work his will.

In other words, Elijah's eyes and emotions gave him a false understanding of what he faced.

The reality of the situation, according to God, was this: Elijah wasn't alone. Though he didn't know it, God had many others in Israel standing for the Lord. But Elijah's emotions had so narrowed his focus that he could no longer see beyond himself.

> Elijah was looking through the eyes of hopelessness instead of the eyes of faith.

God's power was getting ready to enter the picture and take care of his child. But Elijah was looking through the eyes of hopelessness instead of the eyes of faith.

Can you identify with Elijah? If so, then perhaps God is trying to teach you the same thing he taught his prophet.

- Remember: you're not alone; God is with you.
- Keep your eyes on God, not on the circumstances surrounding you.
- God's power can change the situation when he thinks it's time.
- Your heavenly Father will take care of you—no matter what.

STRENGTH FOR TODAY
Your Brain Is the Boss

The brain is the control center of the body. It sits atop the shoulders like Mount Olympus, gazing down upon the muscles, sinews, and guts that comprise us. But, important as the head is, it cannot exist without all the other organs. The Bible draws an elegant corollary: "The body is a unit, though it is made up of many parts; and though all its parts are many, they form one body. So it is with Christ" (1 Cor. 12:12).

The brain communicates with the rest of the body in two ways. Through the spinal cord, the brain sends millions of nerve cells into every part of the body. The body can then send impulses back along these nerve cells.

However, the body can also communicate with the brain through chemicals, or hormones, secreted into the bloodstream. These chemicals have various effects on organs of the body and can tell the brain how everything is functioning.

The body is, in reality, an enormous system of checks and balances. And if something goes wrong with this system, it can give your mind a "wrong" picture of how you are doing emotionally.

This interplay between the body and mind is important to grasp as we examine the physical and psychological aspects of depression. Together, the body and mind determine how you "feel."

In the days to come you will learn how the physical condition of your body can affect the function of your

---

Tools for Tomorrow

LifeFilter 2

How to Have Peace Today
"And the peace of God, which transcends all understanding, will guard your hearts and your minds in Christ Jesus" (Phil. 4:7).

Today

1. Remember: I'm not alone; God is with me.
2. Keep my eyes on God, not on the circumstances surrounding me.
3. God's power can change the situation when he thinks it's time.
4. My heavenly Father will take care of me—no matter what!

---

brain. Also, you will discover how the brain's function can affect the condition of your body. The two are inextricably bound together, and the totality of their balance or imbalance comprises your emotional state.

Be prepared, in the near future, to examine your physical condition in detail. You will perform a health inventory of your bodily condition— information as vital as the psychological condition of your mind. By getting in touch with your physical condition, you will gain more knowledge in the battle against depression.

SUMMARY

"I have had enough, Lord." Have you ever said that? If one of God's greatest prophets, Elijah, voiced those words, you probably have too. But Elijah made two mistakes that allowed him to slip into a negative frame of mind:

1. Elijah's emotions had so narrowed his focus that he could no longer see beyond himself.
2. Elijah was looking through the eyes of hopelessness instead of the eyes of faith.

God helped his prophet through that dark time, and he will help you as well. Widen your focus to see beyond yourself and your problems. Look at your life and this world through the eyes of faith. Open your heart to the possibility of God's beginning a great work in you and giving you blessing after blessing.

PHYSICIAN'S FACT

The brain and body are intertwined in a carefully balanced dance of emotions. Understanding this link will empower you in the future to deal with the mental, as well as physical, changes of depression. _Remember: the body and mind both share the effects of depression._

DAY 3
Finding a Rare Gift You Never Knew You Had

THE POWER TO WIN

Today I'm going to introduce you to one of our crazy ideas: When looked at in the proper way, it is possible to say that our—and your—depression is a gift from God.

Hey, wait a minute! some of you are thinking right now. *Are you crazy? You can't know how much pain my depression has brought me. There's no way it can be a gift from God!* Yet this is a theme Bruce and I will return to repeatedly during the course of this book. We want to show you how to look differently at your depression, begin to see it as a strength, and eventually use it as a tool for good.

How can your depression be a gift from God? You, above all others, are almost forced to find a solution to the problems of life. Others might not question the foundation of their life—until it's too late. You, on the other hand, have an immediate reason for trying to find the way to true peace. Through depression, God has given you the impetus to discover a close relationship with him.

Perhaps the following story will better explain this concept to you.

Linda was pleased with her new condominium. Recently built, the units were attracting people eager to have a quality-constructed home. But as the weeks passed, Linda found an irritating, creaking sound when she walked over one particular area of her bedroom floor. She tried to ignore it, but the sound got worse.

Contacting the builder didn't seem to help; he wasn't concerned. "Every new building has its own particular noises," he told her.

Just to be on the safe side, however, he came out and inspected her apartment. After cutting a hole in the bedroom floor, he examined the support beams to see if everything was in order.

To his surprise, he discovered that the beams which were supposed to join the floor with the supporting wall had actu-

> Through depression, God has given you the impetus to discover a close relationship with him.

ally been cut too short. Not only were they barely long enough to reach the support beams, nothing had been used to attach them!

It turns out that the creaking noise Linda had been hearing was the sound of the beams slowly slipping toward the edge of their supports. What would have happened had Linda not heard that creaking sound? Her floor would have eventually caved in, possibly killing her.

The bothersome noise not only saved her life, but it also saved the lives of other occupants. After discovering the problem with Linda's condominium, the builder decided to check the other units as well. He discovered the same problem in three other units.[1]

When Linda finally realized what was going on, don't you imagine she thanked God for what formerly had been an annoyance?

Can you do the same thing with your depression?

You don't have to say that your depression is wonderful. But can you see it as a constant reminder that you need to stay close to God? If you can do this, *you're taking a first step toward using depression, not letting it use you.*

STRENGTH FOR TODAY
Can Stress Strengthen?

First, metal wires are attached across your chest. Next, a mesh shirt is placed over the wires to keep them in place. Then, you are placed on a treadmill. You begin to walk, the speed steadily increasing in increments. The incline increases, and now you are walking uphill—faster and faster.

Your physician sits calmly at his console, his eyes shifting constantly from you to the heart monitor in front of him. He watches the electrical changes in your heart as it increasingly suffers more and more stress. His end point is simple. He knows you can achieve a certain heart rate safely and go just beyond without causing damage. Only under such stress can your physician be sure your heart is strong enough for life.

When you are suffering from depression, you walk into the valley of the shadow of death. Your world crumbles around you; the sky grows dark. And like the stress test, no one can walk the treadmill for you. Someone, however, is with you. God sits at his console, monitoring your heart.

Dr. Kenneth Cooper, the renowned Christian physician who developed aerobic exercise, has proven the importance of exercise for a healthy heart. It seems like a paradox. Your heart must undergo stress in order to grow stronger.

As much as you may want to avoid depression, recognize that its stress can produce positive growth. Even as you must push your body to its limits in order to strengthen muscles, your emotional state pushes you to extremes in order for you to grow stronger psychologically and spiritually.

Tools for Tomorrow

LIFEFILTER 3

How to Use Depression Before It Uses Me

"But he said to me, 'My grace is sufficient for you, for my power is made perfect in weakness.' Therefore I will boast all the more gladly about my weaknesses, so that Christ's power may rest on me. . . . For when I am weak, then I am strong" (2 Cor. 12:9–10).

TODAY

I will use stress in a positive way to:

1. Examine my relationship with God.
2. Be a reminder to pray.
3. Help me grow stronger psychologically and spiritually.

These concepts are designed to give you hope. They should also help you understand the process of growth better. As the realization dawns that you are growing because of this stress, it will be another important element in your growing knowledge database concerning depression.

Remember, like the physician watching the heart monitor, ready to turn off the treadmill at the first sign of disaster, God has promised he will never give you more than you can handle. Just when you think you can't go on, God will give you the strength to take one more step. We like to think that this book is a part of the strength God is giving you and one way he is saying, "I love *you!*"

SUMMARY

You don't have to say that your depression is wonderful. But we do want you to begin seeing it as a constant reminder that you need to stay close to God. If you can do this, *you're taking a first step toward using depression, not letting it use you.*

PHYSICIAN'S FACT

Today you've learned that repeated stress can produce growth—physically, as well as emotionally and spiritually. In addition, using the principles of today's lesson in dealing with depression can actually heal you and make you stronger! Stress can be turned into a positive force for growth.

DAY 4
Rejecting the Guilt and Embracing the Cure

THE POWER TO WIN

Today, let's get right to the point. There is a sticky question many Christians struggle with: Is depression a sin?

This particular question is posed to me by more people than perhaps any other when trying to understand what is going on emotionally with themselves or with someone close to them. The situation isn't helped by well-meaning Christians who don't understand depression saying things like: "You just need to have more faith," or "There must be sin in your life, or you wouldn't feel like this," or even "If you'd pray harder (read the Bible more, have a deeper walk with the Lord), you wouldn't have this problem." To someone who already feels guilty about everything, this just piles on even more guilt.

But are they right? Is depression a sin, or a picture of sin in our life? I answer that with an unequivocal *no!*

We have already seen that depression can, in many instances, have a physical cause. So can alcoholism and several other things spoken against in the Bible. Follow me closely here: *The tendency toward depression or alcoholism is not a sin; giving in to them, however, is a sin.*

The alcoholic will probably get drunk when he drinks, so the Christian who is an alcoholic and wants to stay in God's will must make sure he never takes another drink. Likewise, the person who has a tendency toward depression isn't at fault if his or her emotions begin a downward spiral. However, how he/she responds to that downward spiral will determine if there is sin.

When I feel depression beginning to clamp its cold hands upon me, I do several things:

1. Above anything else, I make sure I'm still reading my Bible and praying. Depression often makes you want to do just the opposite, but:

- You have the power, in Christ, to do what God wills.

Say no to your emotions and yes to communion with God during these times.

2. I thank God for loving me and bringing me through the bout of depression. This is important. Both of these first two actions go against what I feel. My depression makes me want to stay away from everyone—including God. And it also makes me feel as if no one could really love me—including God. But in reading the Bible, praying to God, and thanking God for his love, I am saying that:

- God's Word, not my present emotional outlook, is my authority.

In thanking God for bringing me through the depression, I am also exercising my faith in God and in his Word, precisely at the moment I don't feel like doing it.

3. I try to keep from making any major decision. I've learned that life looks a great deal more bleak when I'm depressed. Therefore, any decision I make during this time is bound to be colored by a false sense of what's going on in my relationships, my business, and my family.

Taking these steps actually may allow me to have greater faith than many who never experience depression. That's because:

- I thank God for taking care of me and loving me even when I can't feel it or see it.

If that's not a biblical definition of faith, then I don't know what is! For example, look at these verses from the Bible. If, when depressed, you can trust God to take care of you and bring you through your bout safely, then you're exercising faith. If you can believe he loves you even when you don't feel loved, that's faith. In fact, perhaps the person fighting depression who trusts in God has the greatest faith of all! "Now faith is being sure of what we hope for and certain of what we do not see. This is what the ancients were commended for" (Heb. 11:1–2). "We live by faith, not by sight" (2 Cor. 5:7).

So your depression is not a sin in and of itself. But how you respond to that depression will determine if you sin.

> ## Tools for Tomorrow
>
> ### LifeFilter 4
>
> *How to Reject the Guilt and Embrace the Cure*
>
> "The sun shall not strike you by day,
> Nor the moon by night.
> The LORD shall preserve you from all evil;
> He shall preserve your soul"
> (Ps. 121:6–7 NKJV).
>
> ### Today
>
> *I will . . .*
>
> 1. Get rid of the guilt trip and focus on the cure.
> 2. Recognize that depression is an illness that can have a physical basis.
> 3. Remember that God's Word, not my present emotional outlook, is my authority.

Let's try an experiment. Perhaps, when you feel that horrible negative emotion coming on, you usually say something like: "Oh no, here it comes again. I'm in for a horrible time." Next time, however, say this instead: "Heavenly Father, here is an opportunity for me to show great faith and grow in you. May I be faithful to you during this time." It might not stop the depression, but it can surely transform what it does to your life! And it can help you remain true to God even in the midst of emotional storms.

Strength for Today
The Disease Has a Cure

Imagine a world of darkness. In this world your senses are limited to sound, smell, taste, and touch. For most of your life, you have spent every day crouched against a rough, stone wall, surrounded by the sound of a milling crowd. You feel the warmth of the sun as it shines on your face, but you cannot see it. And then a shadow falls across you, bringing welcome coolness. A voice from nearby asks the question you have heard so many times: "Who sinned that this man was born blind? Was it his fault or his parents?"

Paraphrased, you hear, "What did this poor, wretched fool do to deserve a life of misery? Where did he go wrong? What did his parents do that he should suffer like this? What sin in his life has brought him to this life of abject hopelessness?"

PART 1: BUILDING YOUR DEPRESSION-FIGHTING TEAM

Perhaps you have had similar thoughts regarding depression. After all, aren't we meant to be happy and well-adjusted all the time? If we are unhappy, we *must* have done something wrong. In Jesus' day a common conception existed that all disease could be traced to sin. The Savior of the world knew this was not true—and he was getting ready to prove it.

The young man mentioned above, of course, is the blind man from John 9. The questioners were Jesus' disciples. Jesus Christ, with the divine knowledge of the Great Physician, spoke some of the most encouraging words of the Bible: "Neither this man nor his parents sinned, ... but this happened so that the work of God might be displayed in his life" (John 9:3).

"What sin have I committed that has brought me depression?" Many people ask this question. Learn a lesson both from the Bible and from science. Let's paraphrase Christ's words and direct them toward you: "Neither you nor your family sinned, but this happened so that the power of God might be displayed in your life."

I can reassure you that depression is an *illness*. It is a disease with a physical basis. Depression is not due solely to spiritual problems. So get rid of the guilt trip and begin focusing on the cure!

We want to help you find the solution to your depression—the work of God that will illuminate your life and glorify our Creator.

SUMMARY

When you feel depression beginning to take hold of your life, try to do the following:

1. Make sure you're still reading the Bible and praying. You have the power, in Christ, to do what God wills.

2. Thank God for loving you and bringing you through the bout of depression. God's Word, not your present emotional outlook, is your authority.

PHYSICIAN'S FACT

Depression is an illness. It can have causes related to physical illness. In addition, some medications can contribute to a feeling of depression. If you haven't done so, ask your physician about any medicine you are currently taking.

3. Try not to make a major decision while in a depressed frame of mind.

4. Thank God for taking care of you and loving you even when you can't feel it or see it. This exercises your faith and strengthens you.

DAY 5
Beginning to Discover the Real Cause of Your Unhappiness

THE POWER TO WIN

A little girl and her father were on an elevator. After going up several floors it stopped, the door opened, and a beautiful woman got on. The elevator started up again when suddenly the woman whirled around, slapped the father hard enough to knock him down, then got off at the next floor!

Sitting on the floor rubbing his cheek, the man wondered just what had happened. His little girl bent over him and said, "Poor father. That woman didn't like you very much, did she?"

The father readily agreed.

"That's OK," his daughter continued, "I didn't like her, either. When she got on the elevator, she stepped on my toe. So I pinched her!"

It's a fact of life, so we might as well face up to it. Bad things sometimes happen to us when it's not our fault. We can be as careful as possible yet still have no control over the bad actions of others that sometimes spill over into our lives. "But I tell you: Love your enemies and pray for those who persecute you, that you may be sons of your Father in heaven. He causes his sun to rise on the evil and the good, and sends rain on the righteous and the unrighteous" (Matt. 5:44–45).

At what does the above passage hint? It says that good and bad things happen to everyone. Regardless of how you try to control your actions, life, with all its complexity, is going to "swarm all over you" from time to time.

"That's not fair," some wail, never getting beyond being an eternal victim.

"I'm never going to trust anyone, even God, again!" say those who have become bitter because of difficult circumstances.

"I give up. It's useless to try anymore," moan those who have decided to withdraw their energies from trying to live with a positive attitude.

> God hasn't given us the option of giving up, growing bitter, or deciding, in our short frame of reference, what is fair.

Which one of these excuses are you using right now? Or is it yet another I've not mentioned? Whichever one or more excuses you employ doesn't really matter: all of them are wrong. *God hasn't given us the option of giving up, growing bitter, or deciding, in our short frame of reference, what is fair.*

Now take a moment to examine your own attitude. Forget your emotional outlook. If you're depressed at this moment, try to "climb outside yourself" for a minute and look at your life.

Have you given up? Grown bitter? Become a habitual victim?

Confess to God that your attitude has been wrong. Ask him to forgive you and begin changing your attitude, and thank him, in advance, for doing it.

There! If you've done that, you have taken another important step toward a healthy emotional state, regardless of the depression. (Hint: You will probably have to do this more than once, perhaps many times. This is because your outlook on life becomes a habit, and most habits are not broken suddenly. But don't give up; keep on giving your attitude to God.)

STRENGTH FOR TODAY
Take a Health Inventory

I awoke in a cold sweat one night.

Our family was vacationing at the beach. An odd feeling had come over me, and as I looked at my sleeping wife, I had the utter conviction that all I believed in was false. There was no God. I was just biochemistry, and when I died, life would end. I got up immediately and walked to the bedroom where my two children slept. I looked at their innocent features and felt an emptiness so deep it threatened to suck me into some dark, bottomless abyss. I walked out to the ocean and watched the dark clouds churn across a gibbous moon and felt the cold waves wash against my feet.

Where was God?

The feeling lasted only a few minutes, but it shook me to my core. I had never felt such empty, devastating emotions before. In the aftermath I descended into a dark depression.

Weeks later, when I finally discussed the incident with my wife, she pointed out an adverse reaction to medication I had once experienced that left me with similar feelings. Suddenly, I realized I had started taking the same medication just days before our vacation. *The incident was directly related to the chemical changes in my brain from the side effects of the medication.*

> ## Tools for Tomorrow
>
> ### LifeFilter 5
>
> *Physical and Spiritual Attitude Check*
> "Those who hope in the Lord will renew their strength.
> They will soar on wings like eagles; they will run and not grow weary,
> they will walk and not be faint" (Isa. 40:31).
>
> ### Today
>
> *Have I . . .*
> 1. Had a physician check my physical condition?
> 2. Tried to take God's view of my situation?
> 3. Promised God to endure no matter what?

Depression is considered an illness of the mind. However, it can be caused or accentuated by abnormalities of the body. In fact, it can be caused by certain medications.

Part of learning to cope with depression will be a health inventory. Take some time today to stop and look at your health status:

- Do you have a regular physician?
- If so, when was the last time you had a physical examination?
- Are you on any medication?
- Is there a history of depression in your family?

In the coming days I want you to make a commitment to undergo a good physical examination by a physician. If you do not have one, choose a physician who has training in family medicine or internal medicine.

Once you see him or her, do not be ashamed to share your concerns about your depression. Many types of depression are directly related to a medication or a physical condition that can be treated. Also, severe forms of depression may require prescription medication.

When choosing or reacquainting yourself with your physician, view your relationship with him/her as a partnership in treating and conquering your depression. Do not be afraid to ask questions and request that this medical professional spend ample time with you. There are many sources of help for depression in the health field.

With the help of your physician, you can learn more about your current health status and better understand the cause of your depression.

SUMMARY

Take a moment to examine your own attitude. Forget your emotional outlook. If you're depressed at this moment, try to "climb outside yourself" for a minute and look at your life.

Have you given up? Grown bitter? Become a habitual victim?

Confess to God that your attitude has been wrong. Ask him to forgive you and begin changing your attitude, and thank him, in advance, for doing it.

There! If you've done that, you have taken another important step toward a healthy emotional state, regardless of the depression.

PHYSICIAN'S FACT

It is time to get in touch with your physical status. Take a health inventory. *Plan a visit to your physician for a physical examination.* Depression may be related to curable illnesses or to medication you may be taking for other illnesses. Create a partnership with your doctor to help you conquer depression.

DAY 6
Laying a Strong Foundation

THE POWER TO WIN

Several years ago Hurricane Andrew slammed into Florida, killing many people, wounding hundreds more, and causing widespread destruction. In one south Florida town, television cameras recorded a lone house standing firm on its foundation, surrounded by the debris of neighboring houses flattened in the horrific storm.

"Why is your house the only one still standing?" a reporter asked the home's owner. "How did you escape the severe damage of the hurricane?"

"I built this house myself. And I built it according to the Florida state building code," the man replied. "When the code called for two-by-six roof trusses, I used two-by-six roof trusses. I was told that a house built according to code could withstand a hurricane. I did, and it did. I suppose no one else around here followed the code."[1]

Many lives have been built on lots of different foundations. Some are built on money and the acquisition of things. Others are constructed on personal power. Still others depend on the accolades of an admiring public.

When the sun is shining, the breezes are gentle, and everything looks rosy, the quality of foundation you have might not seem important. But when the storms of life hit—when the bitter, cold gales of depression whip against and around you—your foundation had better be sure. Those who bask in the sunshine might get away with not examining their foundation often. But for those of us who walk into the wind nearly every day, keeping our foundation strong and stable is a matter of utmost urgency.

Remember the verses we looked at the first day? Let's read them again: "Humble yourselves, therefore, under God's mighty hand, that he may lift you up in due time. Cast all your anxiety on him because he cares for you. Be self-controlled and alert. Your enemy the devil prowls around like a roaring lion looking for someone to devour. Resist him, standing firm in the faith. . . . And the God of all grace, who called you to his eternal glory in Christ, after you have suffered a little while, will himself restore you and make you strong, firm and steadfast" (1 Pet. 5:6–10).

God's Word is filled with promises for *you*. And these verses are no exceptions. As you read them, believe that God *will* make them come to pass in your own life.

- Being humble is OK; God will eventually lift you up! (v. 6)
- You can give God your anxieties because he really cares for you! (v. 7)
- Though Satan is powerful, resting in Christ means you and God will defeat him. (vv. 8–9)
- Though you may feel weak and incompetent now, God will eventually make you strong, firm, and steadfast! (v. 10)

Now that's what I call a strong foundation! Wouldn't you like to have this kind of assurance in your life? Before this day is over, Bruce and I are going to help you take the first step in having this wonderful future talked about in God's Word.

We're going to help you examine your foundation. If it's bad, we'll show you how to replace it. If it has cracks in it because of neglect, in the coming days we'll teach you how to repair it. And then, together, we'll trust in God to fulfill every one of the promises you've just read.

STRENGTH FOR TODAY
What Is Your Peripheral Brain?

In medical school my white coat was always a mess. Each pocket burst with notebooks, index cards, slips of paper, and pens. These notebooks contained all the minute details I needed to function as a doctor. In the medical profession we call this collection of information a "peripheral brain." Without the notebooks I would have been lost. They constituted my foundation in medical knowledge.

Today I no longer need the notebooks. However, my office is filled with five shelves of textbooks and journals. Contained within these huge volumes is the accumulated knowledge of current medical diagnosis and treatment. I may not remember every minute detail of current medical diagnosis, but I know where to find the answers. When I get lost looking for some trivial bit of medical information or I am stumped by a puzzling disease process, I turn to my library of books, confident the knowledge is there for the taking.

You have taken a big step in fighting depression with the knowledge you have already accumulated. You are building a firm foundation from which you can understand and defeat your depression.

There is more to life, however, than living and breathing. As important as it is to understand your mind and body, you must not forget the impact on your health of the condition of your soul. All three aspects of your existence—body, mind, and soul—are important in the balance of life. Along with the knowledge you have acquired this week, do not forget about the "peripheral brain" living within you: a powerful, all-knowing source of strength in your weakest moments. If you do not yet have Jesus Christ in your life to give you strength and hope, then this day is especially for you. Read on and discover how the Savior of the world can come into your life today.

> ## Tools for Tomorrow
>
> ### LIFEFILTER 6
>
> *How to Make My Life's Foundation Strong and Sure*
> Jesus says, "I stand at the door and knock. If anyone hears my voice and opens the door, I will come in" (Rev. 3:20).
>
> ### TODAY
>
> *I will give Jesus Christ . . .*
> 1. All my fears.
> 2. All my guilt.
> 3. All my mistakes.
> 4. Control of my life.

SUMMARY

We've been talking about foundations—spiritual, emotional, and physical. Before going any further, let's make sure your spiritual foundation is solid. Because without a strong spiritual base to build upon, nothing else you do will have lasting value.

If you have never done so, we invite you right now to give your life to Jesus Christ, God's Son. You can give him all of your guilt, your fears, and your sins. He will take the "garbage" of your life and completely transform it. Christ will forgive your sins—every single one of them (even the huge, terrible ones you don't want anyone to know about). He will begin transforming your fears into hope and giving you the strong assurance you will never again be alone.

Don't, however, misunderstand what we are saying. This is not a one-way agreement. In order for Jesus Christ to accomplish all these things, you must agree to give him control of your life. You must let him direct your life—your habits, decisions, and relationships.

The first part of what we've talked about is instantaneous. Christ immediately forgives and purifies you of all sins. He comes into your life and stays with you forever. He prepares a place in heaven for you that nothing can steal away from you. God adopts you as his child and decides to love you, no matter what, for all eternity!

The second part—letting him have complete control of your life—is a gradual, lifetime experience. The way sometimes may be difficult; at times the path may be hard to find; your faith may falter at certain moments. In spite of all this, however, you will also discover that God's Spirit will guide you to become more and more like the character of Christ.

If you'd like Jesus Christ to come into your life and become the Lord and chief guiding influence, you must: (1) understand you've done some things that are wrong (we call these "sins"); (2) be willing to turn away from these sins (we call this "repenting"); (3) realize that Jesus Christ paid for the penalty of your sins by dying on the cross; and (4) invite Jesus into your life, giving him all your sins and control of your life. How can you do this? Below is a sample prayer. You can either pray it or use it as a guide for your own prayer. The important thing is to understand that Christ is waiting to come into your life right now. All you have to do is invite him in.

"Dear God, I know I've sinned and done some things that are wrong. I also understand that Jesus Christ, your Son, died on the cross to pay the penalty for my sins. At this moment, I am sorry for my sins and want to turn away from them. In the best way I know how, I open my life to you. Please come into my heart, take away all my sins, make me clean and pure, and take me to heaven when I die. God, I give you control of my life, both now and forever.

Thank you for coming into my life. Thank you for forgiving me of my sins. And thank you for making me a Christian. Now help me to live for you. In Jesus' name I pray, Amen."

DAY 7
Relaxing in God's Love

THE POWER TO WIN

Today, we invite you to relax. Relax in the reality of God's love for you.

A museum in a castle at Arstetten, Austria, holds an interesting exhibit aptly titled *Thron oder Liebe*. The translation is "The Throne of Love." The subject of this exhibit is Franz Ferdinand.

Ferdinand was, at one time, heir to the throne of Austria. A problem, however, stood in the way of his happiness. He had fallen in love with Sophie, a young woman who was a "commoner." Permission had been reluctantly given for him to marry her, but he would pay a price for his love. He was told that if he married Sophie she would never be empress, their children could never inherit the throne, and they could never claim the name "Hapsburg."

Ferdinand married Sophie anyway and lived happily with her until his death.[1]

Such is the power of love.

Jesus Christ, God's Son, also gave up a throne. And he did it for you. The cross is God's way of saying, "I love *you!*" How great is this love? When Jesus learned that the price of loving you was to be death on the cross, he said, "I choose the cross."

Such is the power of love.

God's Word puts it this way:

Your attitude should be the same as that of Christ Jesus:
Who, being in very nature God,
    did not consider equality with God some-
        thing to be grasped,
but made himself nothing,
    taking the very nature of a servant,
    being made in human likeness.
And being found in appearance as a man,
    he humbled himself
    and became obedient to death—
        even death on a cross!
Therefore God exalted him to the highest place
    and gave him the name that is above
        every name,
that at the name of Jesus every knee should bow,
    in heaven and on earth and under the earth,
and every tongue confess that Jesus Christ is Lord,
    to the glory of God the Father. (Phil. 2:5–11)

Imagine: Jesus Christ, fully God, allowed himself to become a weak, defenseless baby; he allowed those closest to him to betray and deny him at the toughest point in his earthly life; and, most importantly, he went to the cross and died—all alone. Why did he do all this? Because he loves you! Yes, God loves you, even with your faults and weaknesses!

> Yes, God loves you, even with your faults and weaknesses!

Have you thanked God recently for loving you? Have you ever simply trusted and relaxed in his love?

Take a moment to put aside the distractions of life. Ignore the worries that sap your energy and time. Focus, instead, on your heavenly Father. Concentrate on his wondrous love for you. Marvel on the fact that God sees every one of your faults and weaknesses and yet loves you infinitely more than you will ever understand this side of heaven.

Now, take a deep breath, let it out, and sink down into the marvelous pool of divine love. It is deep enough to hold you, wide enough to encompass you, and pure enough to give you strength, hope, and forgiveness. Such is the power of love—God's love—for you!

STRENGTH FOR TODAY
Brood over the Waters

The Creation account of Genesis contains a curious description. In Genesis 1:2, the Spirit of God is seen "hovering" over the waters. The original Hebrew word translated as "hovering" actually is the concept of "brooding," much as a mother hen might brood over her eggs. The Spirit of God brooded over the waters of a primitive earth. Imagine his power, his majesty, his glory as he gazed down on the chaos of Earth's early oceans!

Waves crashing chaotically in utter darkness bring to mind the conflicting, tumultuous emotions of depression.

Earlier I shared an incident in my past resulting in a profound depression. For years after that incident, I refused to vacation near the ocean. Although I love it, the threat of the resurfacing of those painful emotions kept me from returning. Today, thanks to God, an understanding of my body, a new way of thinking, and LifeFilters, I am better suited than ever to deal with depression. The disease still lurks in the dark corners of my mind, but I have learned that God and I, together, can fight it and win.

When I feel the cold clammy embrace of depression descending, I recall the Spirit of God brooding over the chaotic waters. On that day, God reached down with his finger and, in a creation event mirroring his great love and concern for us, brought life into existence in the warm embraces of Earth's waters.

Tools for Tomorrow

LIFEFILTER 7

Take a Well-Deserved Rest!
"Come to me, all you who are weary and burdened, and I will give you rest" (Matt. 11:28).

TODAY

Remember to . . .
1. Put aside the distractions of life.
2. Ignore the worries that sap my energy and time.
3. Focus on my Heavenly Father.
4. Believe that God loves me, even with my faults and weaknesses.

This summer I returned to the ocean. One stormy evening I stood on the wet sands and watched the same clouds tumble across the horizon I had seen on that fateful night years ago. I watched the same gibbous moon eclipsed by storm clouds. This time, however, I relaxed, stepping into the same waters that were once touched by the hands of God. And as his touch brought life to the earth, it now brought life back into my tortured soul.

Today, relax and reach out with your senses to a waiting God who wants to touch the chaotic clouds within your mind and bring new life, new order, to your soul.

SUMMARY

Jesus Christ, God's Son, also gave up a throne. And he did it for you. The cross is God's way of saying, "I love _you!_"

How great is this love? When Jesus learned that the price of loving you was to be death on the cross, he said, "I choose the cross."

Now take a deep breath, let it out, and sink down into the marvelous pool of divine love. It is deep enough to hold you, wide enough to encompass you, and pure enough to give you strength, hope, and forgiveness. Such is the power of love—God's love—for you!

Part 2

Tools That Lessen Depression: How to Find Them and Use Them

Every professional must know well the tools of his or her trade. The carpenter depends on his saw. The mechanic who cannot use socket wrenches will not be in business long. Any computer programmer worth her salt will know the latest operating system frontward, backward, and sideward.

All these men and women have discovered that having the correct tools and knowing how to use them greatly increases one's ability to get the job done. In the area of depression, the same principle holds true.

Do you have the right tools to fight your depression? And do you know how to use those tools? For the next week Bruce and I will be giving you valuable tools and instructions in how to use them.

DAY 8
Lessons Learned in the Cage

The Power to Win

Let's begin our search for tools that can help you by looking in a rat cage. This unlikely place holds, as you've undoubtedly figured out, rats. The stuff of nightmares and horror films, these animals might be furry creatures, but they're not exactly cuddly. Studying them, however, can sometimes reveal interesting insights about ourselves. So let's open the door and enter the cage.

See those two rats over in the corner? One of them, you'll notice, seems depressed. He (or she, I'm never sure when it comes to rats) became like this because of a series of events in an experiment. Scientists did it by yoking the two rats together in a cage with a wheel on one wall. They gave control of the wheel only to the rat on the left. Both rodents, however, received an identical electric shock. The shock stopped only when the rat on the left turned the wheel.

Now for the interesting part. Though the shock begins and ends at the same time for both rats, it is only the one on the right who gets depressed! Why? Because he has no control over his life. He cannot stop the shocks. Consequently, he quits eating, becomes listless, and shows no interest in his surroundings. The rat on the left, on the other hand, cannot stop the shocks from coming, but he's learned that if he turns the wheel, the pain will stop. In other words, *he has learned that he cannot control when the pain will come in his life, but he can decide how long that pain will continue.*

There's one more lesson to learn before we leave these rats. Scientists have also discovered that if they take the depressed rat on the right and move him to the left—in other words, if they finally put the rat in control of when the shocks will stop—he will never learn the lesson. He has already given up, even when there is a solution at hand.[1]

It's time to leave the rats and go back to our own lives.

> He has learned that he cannot control when the pain will come in his life, but he can decide how long that pain will continue.

This paragraph contains a series of questions I want you to answer as honestly as possible. (Bookmark this page. You might want to come back to these questions and review them from time to time.)

- Now that you're out of the rat cage, are you truly free? Or are you simply in a larger cage of your own making?
- If a solution to your depression is presented to you, will you take it and use it?
- Are you ready to begin controlling how much pain depression gives you, or have you given up?

King David, author of many of the psalms, probably struggled with depression. Listen to what he says in one of his songs to God: "How long must I wrestle with my thoughts / and every day have sorrow in my heart?" (Ps. 13:2a). Can you identify with David? Everything must have looked bleak and hopeless. David's depression was threatening to overwhelm him.

But verse 2 is not the end of David's story. Listen to what this great man of God says at the end: "But I trust in your unfailing love; / my heart rejoices in your salvation" (Ps. 13:5). One of David's secrets is this: he never gave up! He never quit trusting in God, no matter what his emotional state may have been at the moment.

What was good for King David is also good for you and me. Don't give up! Don't, for one more minute, swallow the lie that nothing can be done about your emotional state. With the tools we give you, much of the depression and emotional turmoil you're now facing can be lessened, shortened, or eliminated completely. In the section that follows, Bruce will introduce the first tool that, properly used, can lead to many more practical helps for depression. So get ready to pick up these tools and get to work making your life better!

STRENGTH FOR TODAY
Can You Identify and Recognize Depression? Part 1

Do you remember the rats Mark introduced you to in the first part of this chapter? The rat on the left was able to endure the pain of everyday life without becoming depressed because he had discovered an important tool: *knowledge.* He understood how to stop the pain.

We want to give you this same tool. Depression, properly understood, can be controlled and even overcome. So let's begin with a medical lesson that will help you discover if you are truly depressed. Armed with knowledge, you can begin to open the door of depression's cage and become free.

How do you know if you are depressed? After all, we face down days often in life. What differentiates this blue mood from clinical depression?

The Diagnostic and Statistical Manual of Mental Disorders (Fourth Edition) or DSM-IV is published by the American Psychiatric Association. It is designed to provide standard criteria in diagnosing mental disorders. Below is a summary, in layman's terms, of the diagnostic criteria for depres-

> ## Tools for Tomorrow
>
> ### LIFEFILTER 8
> *The Keys to a Great Future*
> "Brothers, I do not consider myself yet to have taken hold of it. But one thing I do: Forgetting what is behind and straining toward what is ahead, I press on toward the goal to win the prize for which God has called me heavenward in Christ Jesus" (Phil. 3:13–14).
>
> #### TODAY
> 1. I will remember always to trust in God, no matter what my emotional state may be at the moment.
> 2. I will begin looking for someone who can help with my depression.
> 3. I will *not* give up!

sion. Look at each symptom carefully and perform your own mental inventory. Have five or more of the following been present during the same two-week period? Do they represent a change from your previous condition? Is at least one of the symptoms either (1) depressed mood or (2) loss of interest or pleasure? If so, you probably qualify as being depressed.

1. Depressed mood most of the day, nearly every day, as indicated by either feelings of sadness or emptiness, or through observations made by others. In children or adolescents the mood can be irritable.
2. Markedly diminished interest in pleasure in all, or almost all, activities throughout much of the day, nearly every day, as noticed by yourself or by the observations of others.
3. Either significant weight loss when not dieting, or weight gain, or a decrease or increase in appetite nearly every day.
4. Altered sleep patterns—either insomnia or sleeping too much.
5. Decreased physical activity or increased agitation nearly every day.
6. Fatigue or loss of energy nearly every day.
7. Feelings of worthlessness or excessive or inappropriate guilt nearly every day.
8. Diminished ability to think or concentrate clearly or indecisiveness nearly every day.
9. Recurrent thoughts of death (not just fear of dying), recurrent suicidal ideas without a specific plan, or a suicide attempt.

Again, if you fulfill more than five of these criteria, you need to understand that you are clinically depressed. This is the first part of the tool of knowledge—understanding what is going on in your life.

Now for the second part of this tool—knowing where to get help for the problem. Help may come in the form of professional therapy and/or the addition of medication. This is why it is important to seek the input of your physician.

Let me remind you of what we have already discovered: in many cases, depression has a physical cause. Some of you reading this might hesitate to see a doctor. "I can just pray my way through this," you might say. Certainly you need to pray and ask God's help! But there is another aspect to consider.

If you were to break your leg today while out jogging, would you simply say, "I'm not going to the doctor. If I pray and have enough faith, surely it will be all right." Of course you wouldn't! You would probably pray and ask God for faith to get through the ordeal. But you'd also head to the emergency room, get X-rays, then let a doctor set the leg and put it in a cast.

Depression is no different. If there is, indeed, a physical cause, then you need to let doctors "set" your depression and help you get over it. Many Christian physicians feel led by God to use their gifts in order to help people like you and me. Don't deny yourself access to someone whom God may have placed in your path as a tool that will make your life better.

In summary, today you have received three important parts of the tool of knowledge:

1. Knowledge of what the symptoms of depression really are.
2. Knowledge of where you can begin to get help.
3. Knowledge that there are Christian physicians who feel called by God to help you.

Make a commitment now to call someone who can help you.

SUMMARY

King David, author of many of the psalms, probably struggled with depression. Listen to what he says in one of his songs to God: "How long must I wrestle with my thoughts / and every day have sorrow in my heart?" (Ps. 13:2a).

Can you identify with David? Everything must have looked bleak and hopeless. David's depression was threatening to overwhelm him.

But verse 2 is not the end of David's story. Listen to what this great man of God says at the end: "But I trust in your unfailing love; / my heart rejoices in your salvation" (Ps. 13:5).

One of David's secrets is this: he never gave up! He never quit trusting in God, no matter what his emotional state may have been at the moment.

PHYSICIAN'S FACT

Today you have received three important parts of the tool of knowledge:

1. Knowledge of what the symptoms of depression really are—read and apply them.

2. Knowledge of where you can begin to get help—the medical community treats and heals medical problems.

3. Knowledge that there are Christian physicians who feel called by God to help you—make an appointment to see one.

What was good for King David is also good for you and me. Don't give up! Don't, for one more minute, swallow the lie that nothing can be done about your emotional state. With the tools we give you, much of the depression and emotional turmoil you're now facing can be lessened, shortened, or eliminated completely.

DAY 9
The Tool of Knowledge Versus the Fear of the Unknown

THE POWER TO WIN

Have you ever been scared?

Each of us has been afraid of something at one point in our life. When I was a small child, my bedroom contained unknown terrors at night. The closets that held my clothes and toys in the daytime became, with the setting sun, caverns where dwelled . . . Something Horrible. I didn't know what it was. I never saw it, but my imagination told me that if I ever closed my eyes, IT would pounce!

With the passing of years, my bedroom no longer holds those unknown terrors. Now I'm the one trying to comfort the fears of young ones in the bedroom down the hall. But the principle of the unknown still holds true for all of us: That which we cannot see and do not understand holds the power to terrorize us.

That is why the tool of knowledge that you, Dr. Hennigan, and I are constructing is so important. Depression can be terrifying to the person overwhelmed by hopelessness, guilt, and despair. Once the mask of this disease is ripped off, however, it becomes far easier to deal with and live with. Again Bruce and I speak from ongoing personal experience.

Can you identify with the small boy in his bed one night when a violent storm began? As the lightning flashed and the thunder rolled outside his window, the boy began to cry out for someone to help. Just down the hall, the father smiled and shook his head. He knew there was no danger. Trying to calm his son, he said, "Don't worry; you're not alone. You know God is right there in the room with you."

A moment of silence passed, then lightning and thunder shook the sky. The father heard his boy cry out again. This time the boy said, "Daddy, I know God is here with me. But right now I need someone who has skin on!"

> That which we cannot see and do not understand holds the power to terrorize us.

This small child needed someone he could see, feel, and trust, who could take away the terror of the unknown and the nightmares of his imagination.

That's what we are attempting to do for you during these days together. We want you to learn all the symptoms of a depression that may frighten you because you do not understand it. We want to take away the mystery—and the terror—of depression. We want to help you, our teammate, continue to build this wonderful tool of knowledge. With it, you will construct a lifestyle and a mental attitude that can hold the beast at bay.

Before we leave this section, let's return to the story about the boy for a moment. Did you know that Jesus Christ is God with "skin on"? If you desire to know more about the character of God, look at the life of Jesus Christ. He is the One who healed the lepers, cared about the social outcasts, gave a prostitute both forgiveness and dignity, and wept over the sins and hurts of all of us.

Look at what happened to one man who came to Jesus: "A man with leprosy came to him and begged him on his knees, 'If you are willing, you can make me clean.' Filled with compassion, Jesus reached out his hand and touched the man. 'I am willing,' he said. 'Be clean!'" (Mark 1:40–41).

Looking for a God with "some skin on"? Then look again at those words, "Filled with compassion." Come and give your fears, guilt, and hopelessness to Jesus. As he looked at the outcast leper, he will look at you. As you ask for help, Christ, filled with compassion, will say, "I am willing. Be clean!"

Who knows? Perhaps God has intended to use this book as his means of beginning to heal you of depression. This is the prayer Bruce and I pray for you.

STRENGTH FOR TODAY
Can You Identify and Recognize Depression? Part 2

One of my favorite destinations for relaxation and play is south Florida. I can tell you exactly how to get there from my front door. In fact, from my hometown in northern Louisiana, you can drive on an interstate highway all the way to Orlando, Florida. Get out the sunscreen, and put on your sunglasses. We're going on vacation!

At the first intersection with I-49, take a right going south. As you increase your speed, notice how quickly the trees and pastures whiz past. Isn't it great being able to stay on the interstate! Before long, you pass beneath an overpass where another intersecting road crosses your pathway. In fact, during the first hour of your journey, you pass under a dozen such intersections, each connecting to a road that leads to a different destination. Fortunately, since you are on the interstate, you do not have to slow down for these intersections. You continue to speed right along beneath each overpass without even blinking an eye.

> The bridges are damaged because of a deficiency in a chemical such as serotonin.

As you near south Louisiana, you make a turn eastward onto I-10. Until this moment the journey has been smooth and uneventful. No difficulties have hampered your progress. Your speed is perfect, and you anticipate arriving in south Florida by nighttime. You dream of awakening the next day, refreshed and rested, ready to hit the beaches.

Your reverie is suddenly interrupted by a detour sign. It seems that at the upcoming intersection, a portion of the highway is missing just beneath the bridge. All traffic is being routed up the off-ramp, through a stoplight, and back down the on-ramp onto the interstate. You slow down, waiting behind other cars. Tension mounts as the speed decreases. Finally, after what seems an interminable delay, you pass through the stoplight at the top of the overpass and make your way down the on-ramp and back onto the interstate. In moments you leave the broken intersection behind, already delayed on your journey.

Then things begin to get worse. As the next overpass appears in the distance, you notice a line of cars slowing down. Just as on the previous

45

intersection, the highway is once again damaged beneath the overpass. This time, you wait in line for ten minutes. Ten minutes to traverse one hundred feet. Ten minutes delayed all because ten feet of highway is missing!

Soon, you realize your journey eastward contains a damaged segment at each and every overpass! Your speedy journey has suddenly slowed to a crawl. A fifteen-hour drive has now become a nightmarish journey of unknown length. At this rate you may finally arrive in Florida, but it will take your entire vacation!

Think of the interstate system I've just described as an interior map of *you*. A complicated, intersecting system of nerve cells connects your mind to your body. At the intersection of the axon— or nerve "highway"—with other axons, there is an overpass: an intersection where two cells almost touch. The bridge between them, like the ten feet of concrete in the intersection, comes about because of the presence of a chemical called a *neurotransmitter*. This chemical provides the connection between the long stretches of nerve highways.

> ## Tools for Tomorrow
>
> ### LifeFilter 9
>
> *Crossing the Chasm from Fear to Faith*
> "So do not fear, for I am with you; do not be dismayed, for I am your God.
> I will strengthen you and help you; I will uphold you with my righteous right hand" (Isa. 41:10).
>
> ### Today
>
> 1. I refuse to let the fear of depression terrorize me anymore.
> 2. There are physical and emotional reasons for my depression that can—and will—be overcome.
> 3. I will be patient as the repair work is being completed.

In depression, these bridges become damaged, just as in the interstate illustration. The bridges are damaged because of a deficiency in a neurotransmitter made, not of concrete, but of such chemicals as serotonin. The nerve impulse that drives your body, that is the core of your thinking, that allows you to feel, is slowed down to such a degree that all the "traffic" grinds to a near halt. So you can begin to see how the levels of these neurotransmitters is the key to the cause of depression.

What can cause a change in these levels? What breaks the ten-foot connection at the overpasses?

The causes for depression are numerous. For example, depression can be inherited: in these cases, an inborn genetic problem of abnormal neurotransmitter levels is passed from generation to generation. Depression also can be caused by other chemical imbalances in the body brought on by disease states such as chronic illness or altered endocrine function. A classic example is hypothyroidism, a state in which your thyroid gland decides to take a siesta and the rest of the body and mind follow suit.

A number of special situations are associated with depression. These are conditions associated with childbirth, advanced age, adolescence, child abuse, drug and alcohol abuse, and gender. Sometimes the underlying cause is never discovered.

As we explore the nature of depression in the coming days, we will touch on some of these special cases. But for now recognize that just as it takes time to repair the broken roadway before traffic flow can be restored, it takes time to restore the proper balance and level of your neurotransmitters. Sometimes you have to remind yourself of this when you're waiting in line for the traffic to clear. Be patient as the repair work is being completed!

Your tool of knowledge is becoming more complete. And as your base of knowledge expands, you will become more and more proficient at using this marvelous tool to overcome a disease that may have been unfamiliar to you.

SUMMARY

The principle of the unknown still holds true for all of us: *That which we cannot see and do not understand holds the power to terrorize us.* That is why the tool of knowledge that you, Dr. Hennigan, and

PHYSICIAN'S FACT

1. A complicated, intersecting system of nerve cells connects your mind to your body. At the intersection of the axon—or nerve "highway"—with other axons, there is an overpass, an intersection where two cells almost touch.

2. The bridge between them comes about because of the presence of a chemical called a *neurotransmitter.*

3. In depression these bridges become damaged because of a deficiency in a neurotransmitter such as serotonin.

4. In other words, depression can have a biochemical root. The more you understand how chemicals and hormones work in your body, the better prepared you'll be to overcome depression.

I are constructing is so important. Depression can be terrifying to the person overwhelmed by hopelessness, guilt, and despair. Once the mask of this disease is ripped off, however, it becomes far easier to deal with and live with.

We want you to learn all the symptoms of a depression that may frighten you because you do not understand it. We want to take away the mystery—and the terror—of depression. We want to help you, our team-mate, continue to build this wonderful tool of knowledge. With it you will construct a lifestyle and mental attitude that can hold the beast at bay.

DAY 10
How Others' Needs Can Help Your Needs

The Power to Win

Pulling into the fast-food restaurant, I saw something unusual. Five telephone repair trucks dotted the parking lot. Either Hardee's was experiencing major telephone difficulties, or the drivers had decided to take a coffee break together. But what caught my attention were the bright orange cones—the kind usually seen at highway construction sites—sitting behind each truck. The men could not have backed out without crushing them.

Inside the restaurant the men were sitting around a small table, talking and laughing. I ordered my food. Then, on the way past their table, curiosity finally got the best of me.

"Excuse me," I said, stopping beside them. "Would you tell me why the cones are behind your trucks?"

One of the men laughed and said, "'Cause we'd get fired if we didn't. It's the rule." Then he added, "Seriously, we can't see very well behind these trucks. Putting the cone directly in our path every time we park forces us to look before we back out."

Another repairman broke in. "Several weeks ago one of our men was driving a truck that carries the big buckets. He had stopped for lunch and put out one of the cones. When it was time to leave, he walked to the back to pick it up. Right beside the cone, under the left rear wheel, was a small boy who had gotten away from his mother just a few seconds before."

The man shook his head. "If that guy hadn't had a cone behind his truck . . . ."

The men finished their coffee, waved to the waitresses, and returned to their trucks. Each went to the rear of his vehicle, looked underneath it, and picked up the orange cone.

Safety. Always.

Where are the orange cones in your life? God has placed them in some specific areas. He wants to keep you from running over that which is sensitive and vulnerable in your heart and soul. Often, however, we decide to take matters into our own hands and begin moving—or even taking away—God's safety barriers. When that occurs, our direction in life, our relationships, and our priorities slip out of control. It's ironic, but the more we try to control our life instead of letting God have the reins, the more our life careens wildly about, unmanageable and dangerous to us.

That's one of the reasons Jesus said: "For whoever wants to save his life will lose it, but whoever loses his life for me will save it" (Luke 9:24).

God is the Master Designer. He knows everything there is to know about our bodies, minds, and emotions. He knows things about us science has not yet even dreamed of. So it stands to reason that we should abandon control of our life, giving it totally to him who loves us. In doing so, we allow God to fulfill his promise to us. And we can be sure that the "saving" he speaks of is a salvation that spreads into every nook and cranny of our being.

If we are going to give ourselves completely to Christ, then we will begin living as he lived. Christ's purpose will become our purpose. The way he spent his life should be the way we spend our lives. And as we do this, the "orange cones of safety" begin appearing in the right places, protecting us from the world's evil and from ourselves.

As we give ourselves to him, one of Christ's most effective tools can become a part of our workshop. It is the tool of selflessness. Jesus Christ, God's Son, gave himself for others. As his children, we should do the same. I believe it is no accident that the One who spoke of giving us an "abundant life" also spoke of spending our lives for others.

Sacrifice brings security. Meeting others' needs meets our needs. Doing God's deeds in God's name defeats our depression.

The tool of selflessness is not meant to gather dust in our workroom. God reminds us that if we attempt to hold on to this tool it quickly rots, becoming ineffectual. It is only in giving selflessness away that we gain use of and benefit from it.

How does the tool of selflessness work? It's quite simple. We can't truly focus on more than one issue at a time. If we concentrate on looking around us for people to help, we can't be looking at our own problems. If we spend time and effort working to repair the wounds in others' lives, we won't be guilty of navel gazing. And alleviating the fears of those in difficult circumstances means our fears are more likely to disappear because of the little attention paid to them.

1. Let go of the controls of your life and give them to God.
2. Follow Christ's example of helping those in need.
3. Allow God's orange safety cone to protect both you and the lives of others.

Remember: Safety. Always.

STRENGTH FOR TODAY
Is There a Doctor in the House?

Between my junior and senior years of medical school, I worked in the pulmonary medicine clinic. We treated various types of lung diseases, such as emphysema, lung cancer, and asthma. On a hot August afternoon I examined a young woman having difficulty adjusting her asthma medication levels. The medicine she was taking had to be administered in such large doses that she became toxic to the point of vomiting up the dose she had just taken—often before it could take effect. She was frustrated because all she wanted was to breathe.

Throwing the weight of my idealistic young mind into the problem, I came up with the perfect solution. Her medication was available in the rarely used form of suppositories. Granted, the method of administration was less pleasant than the oral route, but nausea would not cause problems with the medication, allowing the dosage to help her breathe.

Beaming proudly with youthful ardor, I handed her the new prescription and asked that she return the next week.

A week later, I entered the examination room expecting to see a transformed woman. Instead, to my horror, I found my patient's asthma so out of control she would require hospitalization to reverse a rapidly deteriorating pulmonary condition! I was shocked and dismayed as I listened to her wheezing.

> Out of necessity, medical treatment is now a true partnership between the doctor and patient.

"Did you take the suppositories as I directed?" I asked.

"Yes, doctor," she replied. "I put one up each nostril just like I was supposed to."

I hope you realize suppositories are not administered through the nasal route. But, to this woman, whose problem was her breathing, putting the medication up her nose made perfectly good sense. The failure in her care was mine, not hers. I failed to communicate properly with my patient. But the patient also had a responsibility for taking control of her care.

As you enter into the healing process of your depression, I want to help you choose a physician and learn to avoid the pitfalls of poor communication.

Communication, first and foremost, is a two-way street. It is as important for a physician to communicate clearly your treatment as it is for you to know which questions to ask. In today's medical climate, patients must become active in their own medical care. The days of "I'll do whatever you tell me, doctor, because I trust you" are gone. Out of necessity, medical treatment is now a true partnership between the doctor and patient. For example, it seems new treatments surface weekly on the daytime talk shows before doctors can learn about them. And with managed care, the new way of dispensing medical care, doctors have less and less time to spend talking to each patient.

For these and other reasons, it is important that you insist on quality time and quality communication with your doctor. Otherwise, your concerns may get swept under the rug in the pressure your doctor feels to see as many patients as possible in a short period of time. You must understand that now, more than ever, some medical care is becoming like an assembly line. Therefore, you must assume a proactive role in your own care.

A new term in today's medical vernacular is *primary care* physician. The primary care physician is on the front line of your medical care and is considered the first physician you should see. A child would see a pediatrician; a woman an obstetric/gynecologist, or, generally, an internal-medicine physician or family practitioner. Most insurance programs, HMOs, and managed-care programs require you to have a primary care physician.

What about more specialized care for your depression? Should you see a psychologist or counselor first?

In most cases you need not worry. Primary care physicians are trained to recognize and treat depression. But you may have to insist on being referred for more specialized treatment under a psychiatrist, psychologist, or professional counselor.

How do you avoid the trap of the suppository up the nostril? In choosing a primary care physician, it is of paramount importance to feel you can develop a relationship with this physician. If you cannot, then find another one. Never be afraid to change physicians or to insist on all of your questions being answered. It is *your* body and mind. Take care of yourself and be firm in your insistence on quality communication. As a doctor, I can tell you most physicians today welcome involved, proactive patients who insist on investing time in their own treatment.

Once you have found a physician, then begin to ask questions. Make a list and insist on the doctor's taking the time to answer all of them thoroughly. Remember, there are *no* "stupid" questions. Every question is valid if you don't know the answer.

> ### Tools for Tomorrow
>
> #### LIFEFILTER 10
>
> *Trusting God and Helping Others*
> "I will say of the LORD, 'He is my refuge and my fortress, my God, in whom I trust'" (Ps. 91:2).
>
> #### TODAY
>
> 1. I will look for someone to help.
> 2. I will begin to look for a Christian physician to partner with me in overcoming depression.
> 3. I will thank God for loving me and being my constant partner.

The most important question to ask your doctor is: "Do I have a treatable medical condition that is causing me to feel depressed? If so, what is the treatment?"

If you do not have an underlying medical condition, here are some questions you can ask your doctor:

- Do I need medical treatment, counseling, or both?
- How safe is the medication you would give me?
- What are the side effects?
- How long will it take for me to see improvement?
- Are there alternatives if this medication proves unsuccessful or has undesirable side effects?
- Will this medication interact with other medications I am taking?
- How will medication affect other medical conditions I have?
- How soon will I feel better?

Every good doctor hopes for willing patients who are involved in their own treatment. Two-way communication is essential to your success. Don't be afraid to be strong. In doing this, you are continuing to take charge of depression instead of letting it take charge of you.

PHYSICIAN'S FACT

1. A doctor is essential in eliminating any underlying medical cause of depression.

2. The doctor-patient relationship must be a trusting, communicating relationship.

3. There are *no* "stupid" questions.

4. Take charge of your own self-care; be proactive. Your doctor will welcome it.

5. Make a list of questions before you see your doctor and ask *all* of them.

SUMMARY

As we give ourselves to him, one of Christ's most effective tools can become a part of our workshop. It is the tool of selflessness. Jesus Christ, God's Son, gave himself for others. As his children, we should do the same. I believe it is no accident that the One who spoke of giving us an "abundant life" also spoke of spending our lives for others.

Sacrifice brings security. Meeting others' needs meets our needs. Doing God's deeds in God's name defeats our depression.

DAY 11
How to Make Progress through Review

THE POWER TO WIN

We are now eleven days into our battle against letting depression control our lives. As a team, we have decided to change our attitude about this pernicious disease and begin overcoming it. The tool of knowledge we've been constructing is becoming more and more complete. And in a few minutes, Dr. Hennigan is going to take us on a fantastic voyage that will show us how to stop depression! But before we do this, let me tell you one of my favorite stories.

There was once a farmer who had a successful dairy business. One day his neighbor came to see him. "Would you mind lending me some rope for a few days?" he asked.

The dairy farmer was busy with his cows. But he stopped what he was doing and answered, "I'd love to, but I can't. I have to use the rope to tie up my milk."

Startled, the neighbor said, "You know that doesn't make any sense!"

The dairy farmer nodded in agreement and explained, "I know it doesn't. But when you don't want to do something, one excuse is as good as another!"

"When you don't want to do something, one excuse is as good as another."

With those words in mind, be honest as you answer these questions:

1. Are you reading a chapter in this book every day? Why or why not?
2. Have you begun praying to God every day? Why or why not?
3. Are you beginning to believe that God really loves you, as he promises in the Bible? Why or why not?
4. Have you made an appointment with a physician about your depression? Why or why not?
5. Are you using your LifeFilters every day as a positive reminder? Why or why not?

I am not pressing you on these questions in order to add to any load of guilt you already carry. Nor do I want you to feel even more depressed because you can't answer yes to all of the questions! But Bruce and I both know what it is like to be depressed. And we know that that state of emotions can paralyze your decision-making ability if you're not careful.

It's easy to make excuses as to why you've not taken the steps recommended already in this book. But be honest; could your reason for not doing it be the same as the dairy farmer's? If so, consider this another starting point and ask God to give you the strength to begin taking the steps to overcome depression.

Again, we know ourselves during depression. We have a tendency to stay frozen in one spot, physically and emotionally. But we must continue to remember that *doing nothing different produces nothing different.*

That's where the importance of today's tool comes in. "Review" is a powerful tool we often overlook. It is easy to get caught up in each day's emotions and activities. If we're not careful, we can find ourselves becoming swept up and moved far from the goals we had originally set. When we take the time to review, however, we force ourselves to take a long look at where we've gone over the previous days or weeks. It helps us gain perspective and make midvoyage course corrections before we go too far astray. The tool of review also helps us realize the progress we've made since the beginning of this book.

After having read the previous paragraph, use the tool of review and take another look at the list of questions. Use them to put your life back on track and to evaluate your progress. And if you see that progress, no matter how small, truly has been made, then thank God for the help and give yourself a congratulatory pat on the back. You deserve it!

Let's close with a reminder from God to all of us about how much he loves even the weakest of us. In this passage God is the shepherd; we are the sheep. Perhaps some of you feel like a baby lamb who is so weak he or she cannot walk one step farther. When you look around at other people, often they seem to be strong and incredibly gifted. You might also wonder how God could love you when he has so many able servants.

What does God have to say to someone like you in these circumstances? "He tends his flock like a shepherd: / He gathers the lambs in his arms / and carries them close to his heart" (Isa. 40:11a).

If you feel so feeble that you cannot walk another step in life, rest in the assurance that God is carrying you close to his heart right now. He has a special love for those who are weak and hurting but who still love him in spite of their difficulties.

You might want to bow your head in this moment and thank God for his mighty love for you.

STRENGTH FOR TODAY
What about Meds?

As a child, I marveled at a movie in which a submarine containing scientists was miniaturized and sent on a "fantastic voyage" into the body of a dying scientist. In order to understand how antidepressant medications function, let's use our imaginations to take a similar journey. Grab your lunch and fasten your seat belts. We're going on a fantastic voyage!

The first thing you notice as we enter the brain area is the perfectly clear fluid in which our submersible is traveling. You are looking through what is called "cerebrospinal fluid." This mixture of water, chemicals, and oxygen sustains and maintains the function of the nerve cells. Look to your right. See that tangle of brown ropes? It looks sort of like the chewing gum you stepped on last week, including the little tentacles that stretched from the bottom of your shoe to the street. If you look closely, you will see millions of these bizarre shapes floating in the fluid, each one with dozens of tentacles stretching out in all directions toward one another. What you are looking at are *neurons;* each of its tentacles is called an *axon.*

See that sudden flash? It looked like lightning, didn't it? In reality, it was a flicker of light coursing down an axon. You've just witnessed the propagation of a nerve impulse. Now watch closely where one axon meets another. Did you see the flicker jump from one axon to another?

Let's move our submersible right next to two adjoining axons. To get a better look at them, let's fire up the molecular magnifier. Screen on! Look at the view now. See how each axon is actually an appendage containing fluid and chemicals? It's sort of like panty hose filled with root beer-colored Jell-O. (Sorry! I forgot some of you have weak stomachs.) Look closely, and you will see tiny pores in the end of the axon.

Now it's time for some hands-on experience. Let's take this thin piece of plastic and go outside the ship. Swim over to the spot where there are two axons right in front of you: the end of one and the beginning of another. Now take the paper-thin piece of plastic and slide it between them. Congratulations, you did it! That means there is a gap between the two axons that is so small it is almost nonexistent. This gap is called a *synapse.*

Now turn on the molecular magnifier in your helmet and take a closer look at the synapse. See those tiny holes in the end of the axon? Watch them closely, because here comes another spark of electricity. Continue to watch as it gets near the end of the axon. There, gushing out of the pores. See the glowing chemicals? Now watch the electric impulse.

"Snap!"

See how the impulse jumps from one axon to the next through the chemical cloud? Congratulations. You have just witnessed a nerve impulse traveling from some higher-function brain cell to another.

Right now we'd better back up a bit, or we'll be swept up in the swirling dots of green coming toward us. Their job is to gobble up the cloud of chemicals. These dots are "enzymes" that clear the chemical, or neurotransmitter, from the synapse. If this weren't done, the axons might become short-circuited, allowing unwanted impulses to race around the brain in total confusion.

Swim this way and examine with me what looks like a "sick" synapse. Here comes a nerve impulse toward it. Watch carefully, and you will notice only a small cloud of chemicals issues from the pores. Too bad! That means there isn't enough of the chemicals to allow the impulse to jump the gap. And that can lead to depression.

Let's try to fix it. Wouldn't it be wonderful if we could cure this person of depression right now! Remember how we had problems with the interstate a couple of days ago? Think of us as the synapse highway repair team. But how can we get these neurotransmitters to do their job? The simplest way is to put up what I'll call "blockades" around the synapse. OK, team, help me spread them out.

Why are we doing this? So that the enzymes will be blocked off. Watch as the enzymes try to get through the blockade to gobble up the neurotransmitters. But it looks as if we've been successful! The blockade has held them off.

I see some of you want to know what these blockades are made of. They've been constructed from antidepressant medication. Now, when the next impulse comes along, there will be extra neurotransmitters left behind to help the nerve impulse make the proper connection.

A quick glance at my air gauge tells me our oxygen is beginning to run low in the survival suits. Let's return to the submersible and review our findings over a minisub sandwich (sorry, couldn't resist).

Antidepressant medications work by blocking the enzymes that clear out the neurotransmitters. In this way necessary chemicals such as serotonin actually increase their level, repairing the damaged synapse. Why are there so many different antidepressants? Because each medication

59

may act on the same neurotransmitter, but each also has a subtly unique action.

This is probably one of the most unique settings you've ever had for eating lunch. It's time now, however, to stop and digest what you've learned. Tomorrow we will begin to investigate the different types of antidepressants and their unique personalities as we continue our fantastic voyage into the realm of medical treatment.

PHYSICIAN'S FACT

1. Learning about depression can be a "fantastic journey" that helps you better understand what is happening inside your body.
2. Depression can have a biochemical root. The more you understand how chemicals and hormones work in your body, the better prepared you'll be to overcome depression.
3. Certain groups of people have a higher incidence of depression than others. If you discover you are in one of these groups, sharing with others your common struggles and victories can give both you and them strength and hope.

SUMMARY

We've made today a "review" day. As you work through this book, it's easy to forget the subjects covered already. Go through the list below one more time. Have you already begun to work through most items on the list? If so, congratulations! You are making some significant progress in your fight against depression. If you've not yet accomplished everything, don't put any additional guilt on yourself because of it. Instead, use the list as a motivator to continue improving your mental, physical, and emotional outlook.

1. Are you reading a chapter in this book every day?

2. Have you begun praying to God every day?

3. Are you beginning to believe that God really loves you, as he promises in the Bible?

4. Have you made an appointment with a physician about your depression?

5. Are you using your LifeFilters every day as a positive reminder?

DAY 12
The Calming Effect of Meditation: Prayer and Bible Study, Part 1

THE POWER TO WIN

What is the purpose of a good tool? Essentially, it is designed to help you do a job that would be much more difficult, if not impossible, were you to attempt to do the job alone. If this is true, then the tool of meditation certainly qualifies as one of the best implements in your entire workroom.

As I begin to discuss this subject with you, however, let me give you a strong word of caution. Meditation by itself can be dangerous. The current trend running through America is that every philosophy, every religion, every person's choice of behavior has equal value. Therefore, the philosophy continues, anything you decide to meditate on will help your sense of inner peace. Bruce and I are convinced that this may be popular, but it is heresy of the rankest form. As my dad used to say to me when I was growing up, "Son, no matter how popular sin is, it's still sin!"

Why do I say it's heresy to believe every philosophy or religion is equally valuable?

First, it makes a mockery of the fact that there are nonchangeable rights and wrongs, no matter what one particular society or culture may say to the contrary. It also ridicules the necessity of Jesus Christ's dying on the cross for our sins. After all, if every religion, every philosophy, and every person's behavior is equally valid, sin can't really be that much of a problem. All one has to do is be sincere, and everything is OK. In such a tolerant milieu the Son of God's death would really be superfluous. And speaking of sincerity, this line of reasoning so popular with many people elevates "simply being sincere" to an unhealthy level. Sincerity won't stop a bullet, keep you from dying if you throw yourself in front of a train, or bring you back to life.

> Sincerity won't stop a bullet, keep the rain off your head, defy the law of gravity, or bring you back to life.

Not long ago a young man from England made headlines around the world because of his misplaced sincerity. He and his girlfriend went to Egypt to visit the ancient pyramids and the Sphinx. There, amidst what he believed were "spiritually powerful" artifacts, he jumped from a high building, sure he would be raised from the dead after falling. He wasn't, of course. Sincerely believing in something that is false will hurt you every time.

Having said this, let me now explain what I mean by "meditation." For you, as a Christian who has chosen God's Word as the ultimate source of authority, it is time spent thinking about what God has said to you in his Word. It is personalizing the promises of God in the Bible. It is listening for God to speak to you and to strengthen you.

In doing this, you begin using the tool of meditation to pry yourself loose from the tyranny of your emotions. Left to yourself, your emotions while depressed will give you a false impression of life, your circumstances, your relationships with others, and God's love for you. Only as you allow God's Word to become the authority for every area of your life—especially when you are depressed—will you begin to correct what is a dark, negative view of life.

When you meditate on the truths and promises of the Bible, you begin concentrating on the world outside your depression. When you meditate on the Scriptures, you allow God's medicine of divine love to flow into your depressed emotions, sending healing and peace.

We will further refine the tool of meditation tomorrow. I'll give you some tips on how to make the best of your time spent in God's Word, and I'll show you why it's important to have a regular system of Bible reading. For now, however, let's close by meditating on these words from God. "The LORD your God is with you, / he is mighty to save. / He will take great delight in you, / he will quiet you with his love, / he will rejoice over you with singing" (Zeph. 3:17).

Each time it is used, replace the word *you* with your own name. Then take a moment to thank God for his mighty love for *you*.

STRENGTH FOR TODAY
Must I Swallow a Pill?

During the Christmas holidays of my internship year, our internal medicine team was shorthanded. An intern fresh out of medical school, I found myself responsible for dozens of critically ill patients. Ordinarily, I had the help of a half-dozen medical students, a third-year "resident" who was two years ahead of me in my specialty, and an attending physician who was a professor in this field of medicine. But all of these members of the team were gone for Christmas vacation. Another intern rotated onto the team for the two weeks, and together we slaved away, caring for our patients until the holidays were over.

> When you meditate on the Scriptures, you allow God's medicine of divine love to flow into your depressed emotions, sending healing and peace.

On the first Monday of the new year, the students returned, along with our new staff physician. Our first order of business was grand rounds, a meeting where we reported the condition of our patients to our new overseeing attending physician.

As my fellow intern presented his first patient, it was obvious he had no idea what was wrong with the man. When the attending physician asked questions concerning lab results, X-ray reports, and therapy, the poor intern sputtered and shuffled his way through index cards without giving any real information. Finally, the attending physician walked quietly over to a window and opened a venetian blind to gaze into the darkening evening sky. We looked at each other in puzzlement, until the intern worked up the nerve to ask what the physician was doing.

"I'm looking for another star in the East," the doctor replied. "It is obvious the only reason your patient has survived the Christmas holidays is because of divine intervention!"

I relate this tale because the development of successful therapies has often been the result of what some may call pure accident but I prefer to call divine intervention.

Would you like to know more about antidepressant medication? Let's join the attending physician on today's grand rounds. You can ask any question since you are a new student exploring the disease of depression.

What about antidepressants? Where did they come from?

Patients need not fear addiction. Antidepressants are not addictive.

Excellent question, my good student. At least you are showing more interest than our bewildered intern. During the 1960s, researchers trying to develop a cure for tuberculosis discovered a class of medication that had no effect on the infection but elevated the mood of ill, depressed patients. By accident the first antidepressants were developed. No star in the East this time, although I would not discount the intervention of the Great Physician.

Speaking of bewilderment, what about side effects?

Ah, yes, adverse effects. If you were to study a good pharmaceutical textbook, you would learn these early medications were not without side effects. But we learned from our mistakes, and they pointed the way toward the development of newer and safer drugs to treat depression. And, let me add, I'm glad you're asking these questions. The more you know about the medication you may be taking, the more you can cope with any problems that may arise.

Our intern seems a bit depressed himself. How do you determine which medication to give?

If we were to examine our intern closely, we would see that he has his own unique combination of symptoms. While all these medications are equally effective, some work better for different combinations of symptoms than others. If the first antidepressant you try does not provide sufficient relief, don't despair. Another probably will. Many depression sufferers must try several different medications before they find the one that works best for them.

Can a patient expect immediate results?

Taking an antidepressant can be frustrating in the short term. Most people experience some unpleasant side effects at first, while the benefits may take four to six weeks to appear. Be patient. Not only will you be rewarded by the alleviation of symptoms with time, but the side effects will subside after a few weeks of using the medication.

How much and what type of antidepressant should we take?

Different antidepressants have different effective dosages. Note that the dose you take has nothing to do with the severity of your depression. Nor does the dose affect your hopes for recovery. The number of milligrams (mg) for an individual medication compared to another is irrelevant. Some antidepressants work at 15 mg a day; others, at 200 mg a day. Don't compare apples and oranges. Recognizing this, be patient, as it often takes a while to get used to taking antidepressants. Most physicians start people on a low dose and slowly increase it over a few weeks or months. Again, having your dosage increased has nothing to do with the severity of your depression or your prognosis. It is a reflection of your individual response to the medication.

Tools for Tomorrow
LifeFilter 12
The Medicine of Divine Love "The LORD your God is with you, he is mighty to save. He will take great delight in you, he will quiet you with his love, he will rejoice over you with singing" (Zeph. 3:17).
Today
1. I will thank God for providing both spiritual and physical medicines that can help me. 2. I will establish and maintain a daily quiet time. 3. Right now I will stop and thank God for loving me.

Can you get addicted to antidepressants?

Good question. Patients need not fear addiction. Antidepressants are not addictive. And the length of treatment is highly dependent on your individual response to therapy. Think of your medication as a diabetic thinks of insulin. You need it to function, and it carries no long-term effects.

If I get to feeling better, can I stop my medication?

Never stop taking antidepressants abruptly. If you do, you may experience serious flu-like symptoms or even a worsening of your preexisting depression. Your physician must taper you off the drug if you no longer need medical treatment.

Well, that concludes our grand rounds for the day. Tomorrow, students, we will go into more detail about the individual types of antidepressant medications. Pay attention. There may be a pop quiz! Good day!

SUMMARY

For you, as a Christian who has chosen God's Word as the ultimate source of authority, meditation is time spent thinking about what God has said to you in his Word. It is personalizing the promises of God in the Bible. It is listening for God to speak to you and to strengthen you.

In doing this, you begin using the tool of meditation to pry yourself loose from the tyranny of your emotions while in the midst of depression. Left to yourself, your emotions while depressed will give you a false impression of life, your circumstances, your relationships with others, and God's love for you. It is only as you allow God's Word to become the authority for every area of your life—especially when you are depressed—that you begin to correct what is a dark, negative view of life.

When you meditate on the truths and promises of the Bible, you begin concentrating on the world outside your depression. When you meditate on the Scriptures, you allow God's medicine of divine love to flow into your depressed emotions, sending healing and peace.

PHYSICIAN'S FACT

1. Medication may be necessary as an accompaniment to counseling for the treatment of depression.

2. Antidepressant medications may need to be tailored to your specific symptoms and tolerance to the side effects.

3. Never stop taking antidepressants or change your dosage without conferring with your physician. The results could be deadly!

4. Be aware of which drugs might interact with your medication.

DAY 13
The Calming Effect of Meditation: Prayer and Bible Study, Part 2

THE POWER TO WIN

Yesterday we began building the tool of meditation. Today we'll learn how to refine and use it properly. We have already established that it is essential for us to read and meditate on God's Word, the Bible.

One of the questions many people ask me is, "How should I read and study the Bible?" It is best to have some system you stay with on a regular basis. Otherwise you could be like this fellow.

A young man once got into some financial difficulty. Looking for advice, he remembered that his dad had always turned to the Bible for inspiration. Not being sure of how to go about it, the young man decided to close his eyes, open the Bible, point his finger at a verse, and follow what it said.

After doing all this, he opened his eyes to see what advice the Bible gave. He was shocked to see his finger pointing at, "And Judas went out and hanged himself." Not wanting to follow this radical procedure, he decided to give his system one more try. This time when he opened his eyes, he read, "Go and do likewise!"

A better way of Bible reading and meditation is to choose several books of the Bible and read a chapter from each daily. Psalms and the Gospel of John are two good places to start. Proverbs gives you some wonderful promises, and 1 and 2 Peter provide divine counseling for living in difficult times.

Some suggestions follow for applying these Scriptures and letting them make a difference in your life:

- Read the Bible daily—even (and especially) if you don't feel like it.

- After you've read a chapter, ask yourself several questions: "What has God taught me in this chapter? What promise has God given me in these verses? How can what I've learned affect my life today?"

- If a verse you've read is especially meaningful to you, write it down and try to memorize it, carrying it with you for several days.

- Take a moment to thank God for his constant love. Pray for someone in need. Ask God to take care of your needs. Tell him of any specific problems you are facing, and trust him to take care of them in his own time and in his way.

Read the following passage from the Bible, then go back to the list and ask yourself the suggested questions about what you've just read.

> Praise be to the God and Father of our Lord Jesus Christ! In his great mercy he has given us new birth into a living hope through the resurrection of Jesus Christ from the dead, and into an inheritance that can never perish, spoil or fade—kept in heaven for you, who through faith are shielded by God's power until the coming of the salvation that is ready to be revealed in the last time. In this you greatly rejoice, though now for a little while you may have had to suffer grief in all kinds of trials. These have come so that your faith—of greater worth than gold, which perishes even though refined by fire—may be proved genuine and may result in praise, glory and honor when Jesus Christ is revealed. Though you have not seen him, you love him; and even though you do not see him now, you believe in him and are filled with an inexpressible and glorious joy, for you are receiving the goal of your faith, the salvation of your souls. (1 Pet. 1:3–9)

How did you do? Did answering the questions help you better remember and apply the passage? If so, plan to use these questions in your future Bible readings.

One of the usual effects of depression is an inability to concentrate and get things done. Simply by reading this book you are fighting those tendencies already! Built into each day are summaries and LifeFilters to help you meditate on what you've just learned. We encourage you to do the same thing with the Bible, God's Word. Taking a daily dose of divine truth will go a long way toward helping you win the battle of depression.

The best tool is useless as long as it is left in the workroom. Take the tool of meditation and begin opening God's Word. It will make a difference in your life. God promises it.

STRENGTH FOR TODAY
Can You Know Your Medication?

During the summer of my junior year in medical school, I spent a week working in a missionary clinic in Mexico. I remember the harsh conditions, the debilitated condition of the patients, and the scarcity of supplies. However, the people we treated had a great spirit. As I saw each patient, I would have to go to our "pharmacy." It certainly was nothing fancy—only a tiny room outfitted with two-by-four shelves. And the only medicines we had were sample drugs donated by pharmaceutical companies. Even though I may have had a specific treatment in mind, I could only choose from the medications available. I remember standing there dismayed at the paucity of choices. Which antibiotic to use? Which pain medicine?

When I visit a pharmacy today, I know the choices will no longer be limited. With literally thousands of medications to choose from, it becomes much easier to select the best one to do the job. On the one hand it can be bewildering to you, the patient. On the other hand it gives your doctor great latitude in tailoring a treatment plan that is just right for you.

Since we are no longer in grand rounds, I will take the opportunity to cover a few of the older and newer antidepressants available for treatment. My purpose is to familiarize you with the names of some of the medications available so you will have the background to ask questions and make a well-informed decision.

All of the antidepressant medications work by preventing the breakdown of the necessary neurotransmitters we discussed previously, essentially increasing the levels of such chemicals as serotonin. These chemicals are necessary for nerves to function properly. In coming days we will discuss the chemical serotonin in more detail.

Nardil and Parnate (MAO Inhibitors). MAO inhibitors are among the older antidepressants. In recent years their popularity has declined considerably because of their side effects, particularly the food restrictions that must be observed while taking them. If you use these medications, you must follow strict dietary guidelines.

Tricyclic Compounds. Tricyclic compounds (TCA) include Anafranil (clomipramine), Asendin (amoxapine), Aventyl and Pamelor (nortriptyline), Elavil (amitriptyline), Norpramin (desipramine), Sinequan (doxepin), Surmontil (trimipramine), Tofranil (imipramine), and Vivactil (protriptyline).

Prozac, Zoloft, and Paxil (Selective Serotonin Reuptake Inhibitors, or SSRIs). The newest type of antidepressant are the SSRIs, especially Prozac.

Wellbutrin and Zyban (bupropion). Wellbutrin and Zyban are among the newer antidepressants.

Serzone (nefazodone). Serzone is in a class of its own and was approved by the FDA in 1995. In addition to treating depression, it also helps treat the anxiety often associated with depression. Relief of anxiety usually occurs quickly, often in the first week.

Side Effects

In general antidepressant medication produces a host of similar side effects. These can include blurred vision, dry mouth, changes in sexual function, sleep disruption, drowsiness, and appetite changes. Not all of these drugs produce all of these side effects. In fact, you may have few or none of them. This is why it is so important to allow your physician to tailor the drug to your specific needs. Some side effects go away with time. Others do not and require changing your medication. In each case your doctor and your pharmacist are ready to help you with the knowledge of your drug's side effects and onset of effectiveness.

Never cease your medication without consulting your doctor, and never change your dosage without consulting your doctor. Antidepressants must be tapered off rather than stopped abruptly. Remember the barrier to the enzymes I discussed earlier? If this barrier is abruptly removed, the neurotransmitters will be depleted so quickly by the dammed-up enzymes that you can have catastrophic results.

If you have questions about specific medications, ask your pharmacist. He can print out an information sheet on the medication. There are also excellent resources on the Internet and in the *Physician's Desk Reference,* the doctor's drug bible available in most bookstores. A note of caution! These sources will list every known side effect, no matter how small the number of incidences. If you're not careful and knowledgeable, the information could frighten you.

Now you see why I place so much emphasis on that relationship with your physician. You are in a partnership with your doctor to defeat your depression. The tools of knowledge and medicine are often effective only if you are using them together.

Summary

One of the usual effects of depression is an inability to concentrate and get things done. Simply by reading this book, you are fighting those tendencies already! Built into each day are summaries and LifeFilters to

PHYSICIAN'S FACT

1. A host of older and newer antidepressant medications are available to meet your specific needs.

2. Antidepressants have different side effects depending on their chemical action.

3. Never stop taking a medication abruptly.

4. Never change your medication dosage on your own.

5. Your doctor and your pharmacist are your best sources for information.

help you meditate on what you've just learned. We encourage you to do the same thing with the Bible, God's Word. Taking a daily dose of divine truth will go a long way toward helping you win the battle of depression.

DAY 14
God's Love—a Place to Relax

THE POWER TO WIN

The couple and their young son were getting ready to order their evening meal at a local restaurant. As the parents asked for substitutions and gave careful instructions for the kitchen on their food preparation, the veteran waitress took it all in stride. She had seen it all and was unflappable. She also had her own ideas about what was right and wrong.

When it was the boy's turn to order, he rushed his words as fast as he could, knowing it was probably futile. "I want a hot dog—"

Before he could say anything else, his parents interrupted, "No hot dog!" The mother began making a substitute order for her son. "Instead, bring him the beef, some vegetables and—"

She stopped in midsentence, her mouth open. The waitress wasn't even listening to the parents. Calmly, without hurry, she looked at the boy and asked, "What would you like on your hot dog?"

He smiled at her shyly and said, "Just ketchup—and lots of it! And please, could I have some milk?"

"No problem," the waitress said as she turned toward the kitchen, leaving behind stunned parents and an incredulous boy.

When she had gone, the boy turned to his parents with a big smile and said, "I like her. She thinks I'm real!"[1]

Do you ever feel like that little boy? You have real longings, unspoken hopes, deep heartaches. Yet when you dare to try to express any of these emotions, perhaps you find others not really listening. Or if they listen, perhaps they are uncomfortable with the subject matter. Instead of taking you seriously and trying to deal with what you've said, they may even try to sweep your moods under a rug, telling you just to forget about them.

You've looked for help. Instead, you've found misunderstanding.

If you can identify at all with what I've just written, then you feel just like many people I counsel. Because they can't take an Alka-Seltzer and feel better in thirty minutes, or get an antibiotic shot and be well in four days, most of society doesn't know how to deal with those struggling with depression. So what happens with many people follows this scenario: (1) There is an initial rush of compassion for the depressed individual from family or friends. (2) Much advice is given with confidence—often from people who have never suffered from depression in their life. (3) When the advice doesn't work (often because it's wrong), or when the depressed individual doesn't "rejoin" society immediately, those who were formerly caring begin to lose patience. They go on with their lives, leaving you to struggle with yours.

They no longer treat you like a "real" individual.

The widows and orphans of Old Testament times must have felt the same way. These two groups were disenfranchised and endangered. They lived in a harsh time when slavery and cruel deaths were common. There was no Social Security to look after these people, no government programs to ease their burden, no media to bring to light their needs. And so these, the weakest of the weak, suffered horribly, often going to an early death. Few were willing to treat the widows and orphans as "real" individuals.

In this context God, with the following words, explodes into the midst of an uncaring society and changes the fortunes of the "forgotten ones." "A father to the fatherless, a defender of widows, / is God in his holy dwelling. / God sets the lonely in families, / he leads forth the prisoners with singing" (Ps. 68:5–6a).

When no one cares for society's outcasts, God astounds us by saying, "I care." Our heavenly Father is a loving, caring parent to all those who never had a good family life. He gives a home with a warm atmosphere to anyone who is lonely. And, finally, God promises to lead you out of your emotional prison and give you joy.

In other words, God cares for _you!_ When no one else pays attention to your problems, know that God is right beside you, caring for _you!_ When it seems that no one can understand the depths of your pain, God is there with perfect understanding, and he cares for _you!_

You and I are like the little boy in the restaurant. We can say, "I love God. He pays attention to me and cares about my needs. _He thinks I'm real!_"

STRENGTH FOR TODAY
Who Are Those Angels in White Coats?

Sharon, a delicate child with porcelain skin and pale blue eyes, lay in the hospital bed staring at the robins nesting on the ledge outside her hospital room window. Her skin was pale because she had a low blood level. Her blood level was low because her bone marrow was ravaged by cancerous cells. She was dying from leukemia.

I remember her face illuminated by the reflected sunlight struggling to pass through the narrow windows of the fifth floor of my teaching hospital. She was so full of life, so full of possibilities. My heart was broken, not so much because she was dying, but because her form of leukemia was curable. We had it in our grasp to save this young girl's life. What was standing in our way?

You've heard this type of story dozens of times. Parents who rely so strongly on their faith to heal their child that they refuse to see any other form of salvation.

How could I reach them? How could I break through this barrier to modern medicine Sharon's parents had erected?

The secret lay in my past. As a senior in high school, my ambition was to become an astronaut—to journey among the stars, seeking out new life and new . . . . Well, you know the rest! I would have happily settled for the job of a chemist, or an astrophysicist, or any scientific position as long as it was _not_ in medicine. The last thing I would ever want to be was a doctor.

In the winter of my senior year, my pastor preached the only sermon I can still remember. He related how God calls *all* of us to work for him. Not everyone is a preacher or a missionary. Some of us are called to be good Christian schoolteachers, godly accountants, or gas station attendants for Christ. The important point is to find where God wants you to be. I was so convicted that I bowed my head and surrendered my future to God.

God spoke to me that day. Not in a thunderous voice from heaven. Not with doves descending or angels singing. In my heart I knew beyond the shadow of a doubt that I was meant to be a doctor. I also found an instant, life-sustaining peace with that decision. As I left the church that cold Sunday morning, I knew where my future lay. There would be obstacles, hard times, and difficulties. But I did not despair. God had decided I was to be an instrument of his healing power.

As I remembered my experience, I sat on the bed next to Sharon and asked her parents to listen to my story. I told them, "You have prayed for God to heal Sharon. If I am called by God as an instrument of his healing, then I may be the answer to your prayer. Will you let God help your daughter through me?"

After praying about it and talking with Sharon, the parents allowed us to proceed with treatment. Somewhere today, twenty years later, I like to think Sharon is showing her daughter the beautiful robins nesting outside her bedroom window.

Shortly before Super Bowl XXXIII, Dan Reeves, the coach of the Atlanta Falcons, underwent bypass surgery for coronary artery disease. Publically, he credited Jesus Christ with his recovery. He said God had sent him "angels in white coats" to heal him. As you prepare to be the

---

Tools for Tomorrow

LifeFilter 14

Understanding God Cares for Me

"Cast all your anxiety on him because he cares for you" (1 Pet. 5:7).

Today

I will remember . . .

1. No matter what I face, God cares for *me!*
2. God also cares for me through the concern and wisdom of other Christians.
3. In other words, I am not alone!

---

victor over your depression, please realize that God can use doctors and nurses and counselors as his instruments of healing. Don't try to do it on your own. Listen to the wisdom of the Holy Spirit and seek out the health-care professional God has raised up just to take care of you.

SUMMARY

When no one cares for society's outcasts, God astounds us by saying, "I care." Our heavenly Father is a loving, caring parent to all those who never had a good family life. He gives a home with a warm atmosphere to anyone who is lonely. And, finally, God promises to lead you out of your emotional prison and give you joy.

In other words, God cares for _you!_ When no one else pays attention to your problems, God is right beside you, caring for _you!_ When no one can understand the depths of your pain, God is there with perfect understanding, and he cares for _you!_

You and I are like the little boy in the restaurant. We can say, "I love God. He pays attention to me and cares about my needs. _He thinks I'm real!_"

Part 3

Three Key Medicines for the Body and Soul

All of us have some definite opinions about medicine. One of the most-voiced comments concerns medicine's expense. For the past several years, my wife has been taking an antinausea drug in conjunction with some chemotherapy. Each pill, taken up to four times a day, costs about $40. That can add up to more than $4,000 a month—just for one medicine! Some people are facing the sad reality that without a good medical insurance program the best medications can be beyond their means.

In spite of this, some of the best medicines in the world are getting ready to become available to you—regardless of how much or how little medical insurance you may have. Over the next three days I'll be prescribing them to you, along with instructions in how to make these medicines work to their fullest capability. Dr. Hennigan is normally the one who writes prescriptions, but in this case I'll be joining him. That's because these medicines are unique: they cost nothing, have no side effects, can be taken all the time with no danger of overdosing, and are guaranteed to help with your depression.

Let's get out the prescription pad and begin!

DAY 15
Laughter: The Wonder Drug

THE POWER TO WIN

A policeman had a perfect spot to watch for speeders, but he wasn't getting many. When he finally peered out from behind the billboard that was his hiding place, he discovered the problem: a few hundred yards up the road a ten-year-old boy held a large sign that read "WARNING! RADAR TRAP AHEAD." Upon further investigation the policeman discovered the boy was actually a young entrepreneur. He had placed a friend just down the road from the policeman with a large bucket in front of a sign that said, "TIPS"—and the bucket was full of money!

Did that make you chuckle? If not, let me try another one.

It happened in church. One Sunday a young couple just couldn't get their little boy to behave. Full of energy, he wiggled and squirmed, talked out loud, and stood up on the pew to look at the people behind him. The parents were doing their best, but they were fast losing the battle. Finally the father decided the child had gone too far. He picked up his son and walked sternly up the aisle on his way out. Just before reaching the safety of the foyer, the little boy, knowing what was coming, called loudly to the congregation, "Pray for me! Pray for me!"

Did you just take your medicine? Did you laugh?

For years, *Reader's Digest* has had a section entitled, "Laughter: The Best Medicine." Science now knows the truth of that statement. Laughter is, indeed, one of the best medicines you can take for your body and soul. In the next section Bruce will tell you exactly how laughter can strengthen your emotions. But for right now just take my word that it really helps you.

One of the characteristics of many of the depressed people I've counseled is that they are what I term "emotionally dead." They don't want to be touched or held. Neither smiles nor frowns cross their face. Their eyes look dull and lifeless. As one woman put it, "In my depression I can't feel anything." Except sadness, of course.

> You can either be sad and wretched the rest of your life, or you can cheerfully feast on what life gives you, instead of letting it feast on you!

I sometimes tell people going through a bout of depression about one of my own experiences. When I'm fighting depression, I can hardly bear to watch the news. The events others watch unfold on the television screen seem mildly interesting to them. For me, however, these same events bring on tears and deepen my depression. An earthquake in Afghanistan? I grieve for the people who lost loved ones. An airline crash in Japan? I begin to realize how difficult life is. A family in Nevada has to file bankruptcy? I find myself crying for their plight and don't know how I can continue in this difficult world.

Interestingly, most depressed people who hear this begin nodding their heads and then say, "You understand!" These individuals discover they are not alone in being unable to deal with the world's news. I believe it's because people who are depressed are under attack and need all their resources to fight off the numbing power of negativity. It is hard to observe the sadness in the world and the sadness in your soul at the same time.

That's where laughter comes to the rescue. It might be good for your general health, but if you take a pill of laughter, the medicine will go straight to where depression threatens your emotional health and begin fighting it. But let me caution you ahead of time: you probably won't feel like taking this medicine. When emotional numbness has paralyzed you, it's easier to sit and do nothing. Remember, however, that we have repeatedly talked about the necessity of going against your emotions to free yourself from depression. It might not be easy, but adding laughter to your life will really help your emotional state.

If I feel depression coming on, I'll often get out a couple of "Pink Panther" movies starring Peter Sellers. They are clean, hilariously funny, and they lift my spirits. Or I might call up a positive friend I know who has a good sense of humor and begin talking with him. Before long I'm laughing, and my spirits have been lifted.

There's another way to take the medicine of depression. It might sound strange, but it really works. If you can't find something funny to watch, read, or listen to, simply smile. You don't have to have a reason to smile. You don't even have to want to smile. Just smile! At first you'll feel a little stupid, but don't worry. Keep smiling, and your body and brain will get the message you've taken the medicine of laughter. They, in turn, will release the chemicals that make you feel better.

Earlier, I said science has finally learned that laughter is a good medicine that has healing power. The Bible has been saying the same thing for more than two thousand years! In Proverbs 17:22, God gives us this prescription for happiness: "A cheerful heart is good medicine."

So, please take your medicine! Remember, you might not be able to choose when or where depression is going to hit you, but you can choose how to respond to it. Don't fear it; fight it! And, yes, you can fight it. Realize that how you choose to respond to depression, according to God, will also determine your quality of life: "All the days of the oppressed are wretched, / but the cheerful heart has a continual feast" (Prov. 15:15). Don't allow yourself to be sad and wretched the rest of your life. Decide to feast cheerfully on what life gives you, instead of letting it feast on you!

Once more, you have a choice. If, as you are reading these words, you are currently depressed, you might feel as if there is no hope for you. But that's not true at all. You always have a choice. Take a moment to bow your head and pray to your heavenly Father. Ask him for the strength to stand up to your emotions and begin trying to bring some cheer into your life. Then, watch something truly funny—not just once but on a consistent basis. If you're not sure what you can find that's amusing, get a Dennis Swanburg video or cassette. Find a Chris Elrod comedy cassette. Get the Gaither Male Vocal Band and listen to Mark Lowery's comedy routine. All of these can be ordered from most Christian bookstores.

Take your medicine regularly, and keep smiling!

STRENGTH FOR TODAY
A Giggle a Day . . .

Garnett awaited the kiss of a charming prince to awaken her from her sleep. Unfortunately, she had to settle for a struggling junior medical student freshly rotated onto the obstetric wards. With her mother hovering over her slumbering form, tucking and dabbing and keeping her body fresh, Garnett gave life to the baby growing within her without ever knowing it. Just four months into her pregnancy, Garnett developed a brain abscess and descended into a coma. Since then she had been admitted to the obstetrics ward for daily intravenous antibiotics while we watched over the child in her womb.

I had an easy job, checking her feeding tube, fine-tuning her intravenous antibiotics, and daily checking on the progress of the baby. The hard job belonged to her mother. Ruby attended to her daughter's needs as a hen broods over her unhatched egg: talking to Garnett daily, rubbing her arms, giving her a bath, and speaking to the unborn grandchild.

On a cold February night Ruby had all she could take. She stood by the window overlooking the roof of the hospital wing next to the ward and watched a raging snowstorm descend upon our city. Her face was drawn and waxen, her eyes downcast and filled with tears, her entire demeanor testifying to the desperate circumstances of her pitiful life. If only there were something I could do to cheer her up.

At that moment cold fire erupted on the side of my face, and I stumbled across the room as another icy missile hit me between the eyes. I fell across a stool and ended up in the bedpan on the floor, covered with snow. Ruby's eyes were wide in shock almost as much as my own as we both looked up to see my attending resident poised in the open window with another snowball in his hand.

Ruby glanced at me, and a miracle occurred. Her eyes lit up with an emotion that had not appeared there in months. Her frown fractured as the muscles of her face contracted in a spasm of uncontrollable laughter. Ruby was laughing. Not just a giggle, not just a chortle, but a deep, restorative belly laugh that shook the walls and rattled the windows. I watched in amazement as Ruby climbed through the window and out onto the roof to engage in a snowball fight with three doctors, four medical students, and one wayward nurse.

The rest of Garnett's medical course was uneventful. After giving birth to a healthy baby boy, she transferred to the medical wards. There, in a twist of "fate," I ended up as her student doctor when I rotated onto internal medicine wards. It took three more months, but Garnett recovered from her coma and walked out of the hospital.

Years later as an intern freshly graduated from medical school, I saw Garnett in the hallway of the pediatric wards with her rambunctious little boy. She smiled at me and patted me on the shoulder.

"I want to thank you for taking care of my mother while I was sick. She still talks about the night you saved her life with a snowball fight. No wonder she gave you that nickname."

I raised an eyebrow in puzzlement. "She gave me a nickname?"

"She calls you Doctor Goofy."

William F. Fry, M.D., of Stanford University, an expert on the physiological effects of humor for thirty years, believes laughter triggers physiological changes in the body that counteract stress. Fry believes laughter induces the brain to release certain chemicals that restore the normal balance of neurotransmitters. In other words, laughter causes the release of more of the helping chemicals in the brain, restoring the depleted chemicals that result in depression. In addition, Fry contends that laughter, like aerobic exercise, reduces the heart rate and blood pressure and causes chest, abdomen, and shoulder muscles to contract, thus relieving stress. Because every brain pathway occupied by the job of

---

Tools for Tomorrow

LifeFilter 15

A Cheerful Heart Is Good Medicine

"If you obey my commands, you will remain in my love. . . . I have told you this so that my joy may be in you and that your joy may be complete" (John 15:10a,11).

Today

I will try to . . .

1. Remember, a giggle a day keeps the doctor away. But it also allows the Great Physician to make house calls!

2. Be joyful because God loves me.

3. Smile at five people, and let God's joy flow through me.

laughing is one less pathway to carry distressing thoughts, laughter serves as a temporary distraction by drawing attention away from the source of mental pain. In fact, we now have evidence which demonstrates that most of the major physiological systems of the body are stimulated or activated during mirthful laughter.[1]

Remember earlier when we discussed the breakdown of the normal synaptic pathways? The overall effect is to slow down the mind and body to a crawl. Depression initiates and maintains inertia. It produces a state of "economy of motion" or the unwillingness to move. Laughter is one way to overcome this inertia.

Rest assured, humor and laughter are more than just an idle diversion. They are therapy. Go to a funny movie. Read a book of jokes. Listen to one of Mark's sermons (sorry, Mark!). Watch reruns of Red Skelton. Do something to give you an opportunity to smile and perhaps to laugh. It will be the first step in the long road to recovery. Or, to reword an old adage, a giggle a day keeps the doctor away!

SUMMARY

Please take your medicine! Remember, you might not be able to choose when or where depression is going to hit you, but you can choose how to respond to it. Don't fear it; fight it! And yes, you can fight it.

Realize that how you choose to respond to depression, according to God, will also determine your quality of life: "All the days of the oppressed are wretched, / but the cheerful heart has a continual feast" (Prov. 15:15).

Don't allow yourself to be sad and wretched the rest of your life. Decide to feast cheerfully on what life gives you instead of letting it feast on you!

PHYSICIAN'S FACT

1. Depression produces a physiological state of "economy of motion" or inertia.
2. Laughter stimulates the mind and body and restores the normal balance of brain chemistry.
3. Laughter can become the impetus to give you the momentum you need to leave depressive inertia behind.

DAY 16
The Transferable Power of Touch

THE POWER TO WIN

Touch is a powerful medicine. Something wonderful happens when one person touches another in love and compassion. It's like a gentle electric current flowing back and forth, affecting both individuals for the better.

Some people are more comfortable with physical contact than are others. I grew up in a family that hugged and kissed one another regularly. In addition, I have an outgoing personality. If I'm around you for awhile and you look like you're sad or depressed, I'll probably try to give you a warm hug. If I see you're uncomfortable with that, I'll at least give you a pat on the shoulder.

In our house Susan and I try to hug each other at least twelve times a day! We do the same with our children. When all three of our daughters were growing up, we would regularly make a "sandwich" of each of them. Jennifer, for example, is our middle child. Susan and I would stand on either side of her and begin hugging each other. Jennifer, surrounded by parents and hugs, would say, "Look, Mom and Dad. You have a 'Jennifer sandwich'!" Over the years we've made Amy, Jennifer, and Sarah sandwiches countless times. Even today, with two of our daughters married, we make "sandwiches" of each of them—and they still love it!

I've given you my background so that you can understand the importance of this next statement. When I'm depressed, I don't want anyone to come near me, touch me, try to hug me, or do anything that I would have to respond to. What has happened to change me so much? I've been infected with the disease of depression. One of its symptoms is a creeping paralysis that, if left unchecked, will infiltrate every part of my body. One of the cures for this is to apply liberally the medicine of touch.

Again, I don't want to touch or be touched. But intellectually I know I must go against my emotions.

Let me remind you that, together, we have learned over the past several days of this book that all of us have the power to choose to act against our emotions. So I allow my wife to embrace me, and I make sure I hug back. Of course, Susan is a canny spouse. Knowing the power of depression, she won't let me go with just one hug. Instead, she will hug me many times more than normal if she sees the numbing flow of depression wash over me.

During his earthly ministry Jesus knew about the tremendous, transferable power of touch. As you read these next words, try to identify with the woman at the heart of this vivid event from the life of Christ:

A large crowd followed and pressed around him [Jesus]. And a woman was there who had been subject to bleeding for twelve years. She had suffered a great deal under the care of many doctors and had spent all she had, yet instead of getting better she grew worse. When she heard about Jesus, she came up behind him in the crowd and touched his cloak, because she thought, "If I just touch his clothes, I will be healed." Immediately her bleeding stopped and she felt in her body that she was freed from her suffering.

At once Jesus realized that power had gone out from him. He turned around in the crowd and asked, "Who touched my clothes?"

"You see the people crowding against you," his disciples answered, "and yet you can ask, 'Who touched me?'"

But Jesus kept looking around to see who had done it. Then the woman, knowing what had happened to her, came and fell at his feet and, trembling with fear, told him the whole truth. He said to her, "Daughter, your faith has healed you. Go in peace and be freed from your suffering." (Mark 5:24–34)

The transferable power of touch. Jesus used it frequently in his dealings with those who were ill.

Jesus touched the blind: "'Lord,' they answered, 'we want our sight.' Jesus had compassion on them and touched their eyes. Immediately they received their sight and followed him" (Matt. 20:33–34).

Jesus touched those who could not hear or speak: "There some people brought a man to him who was deaf and could hardly talk, and they begged him to place his hand on the man. After he took him aside, away from the crowd, Jesus put his fingers into the man's ears. Then he spit and touched the man's tongue. He looked up to heaven and with a deep sigh said to him, "Ephphatha!" (which means, "Be opened!"). At this, the man's ears were opened, his tongue was loosened and he began to speak plainly" (Mark 7:32–35).

Jesus even touched those who were repulsive to society: "While Jesus was in one of the towns, a man came along who was covered with leprosy. When he saw Jesus, he fell with his face to the ground and begged him, 'Lord, if you are willing, you can make me clean.' Jesus reached out his hand and touched the man. 'I am willing,' he said. 'Be clean!' And immediately the leprosy left him" (Luke 5:12–13).

Why did Jesus insist on touching all of these people? After all, he could have healed any one of them by simply speaking his will. I believe it's because our Savior, who knows the heart of his children better than anyone, knew these deprived men and women needed to be healed in more ways than one. When Christ healed them, he did so completely. The blind, deaf, and lame not only became whole physically; Christ also forgave them of their sins and strengthened their emotions. His touch was a powerful part of helping them emotionally.

A mighty warhorse on his way to battle was stopped by the sight of a sparrow in the middle of the road. Flat on its back, its tiny claws pointed toward the sky, the bird made an unusual sight.

"What in the world are you doing?" the warhorse asked.

"Oh mighty warrior," replied the sparrow, "this morning I heard the sky was going to fall."

The horse gave a derisive snort. "Do you really think your pitiful legs are going to make any difference in the outcome?"

Said the sparrow wisely, "One does what one can."[1]

That is all God asks of you and me: to do what we can. The surprising element in all of this is that when we do what we can with what we have, God blesses in surprising ways. Sometimes, to our astonishment, wonderful things are accomplished.

The next time depression begins infecting you, take your medicine: find someone to hug and touch. You may not believe it at the time, but that touch will eventually help heal you of the numbness that holds you fast.

John L. Mason once said, "The best helping hand you will ever find is at the end of your own arm."[2] Use it to touch others and, in the process, heal yourself.

STRENGTH FOR TODAY
Sarah Who?

Let me introduce you to one of my medical school professors: Dr. Molly Cule. She has taught biochemistry, the study of biological chemicals, for years. An unusual teacher, Molly Cule will inundate us with facts and figures, concentrations of this chemical and that enzyme, until we will be overwhelmed. With a twinkle in her eye, she feigns horror that we will be unable to take in any more information.

"Allow me to give you some advice," she says. "You will forget 90 percent of everything you learn in medical school. But don't worry, you really only need about 85 percent of what you learn. Don't waste your time memorizing this minutiae I am doling out. For instance, who cares if the average goldfish gill mitochondria contains fourteen milligrams of serotonin? Ooops!" She places her hand to her mouth in horror. "I've just wasted another one of your neurons. You only have a certain amount, so don't waste neurons on meaningless facts you'll forget right after the next test. Save the neurons for the important facts that can help your patients."

(This lecture actually happened years ago, and to this day I still recall that the average goldfish gill mitochondria contains fourteen milligrams of serotonin. My first introduction to this brain chemical came on the same day I wasted another neuron!)

Serotonin. If you haven't heard about this neurotransmitter by now, you will hear more about it as you battle depression. It is a buzzword on all the television talk shows and pops up frequently in tabloid and magazine articles about depression. Most of the newer antidepressant medications work by their effect on serotonin levels in the brain. Serotonin is so important in understanding and overcoming depression that I would like to discuss it briefly and perhaps use up a few of your neurons.

> Without serotonin, the king of the neurotransmitters, we wouldn't be able to survive very long.

Let's begin by joining Dr. Molly Cule in the biochemistry lab and see what we can learn about serotonin. Our professor is holding a model of two nerve endings very close to each other. Remember the synapse we talked about on our voyage into the brain? As Dr. Cule introduces a chemical substance into the gap between the nerve endings, we see the spark of a nerve impulse jump from one nerve ending to the next. The chemical facilitating the nerve impulse conduction across the synapse is called a neurotransmitter.

Molly Cule is quick to point to a chart listing the benefits of neurotransmitters. They allow us to think, perceive, and move. Serotonin, the neurotransmitter we are most interested in, also controls the regulation

> The balance of the effects of serotonin in your brain and the effects of your environment work together to determine your mood.

of the contraction and expansion of blood vessels; the contraction of the "smooth muscles" of our intestines that aid digestion by pushing food through the gastrointestinal tract; and the function of the "platelets," a component of blood that initiates blood clotting. So, without serotonin, the king of the neurotransmitters, we wouldn't be able to survive very long.

Now Dr. Molly Cule is pointing to a diagram of the brain and its connections to the spinal cord. See the long set of nerve cells that extends from the brain all the way out to the body? These nerves are called the "serotonin system," and they extend from the brain to the body, composing the single largest system in the brain. This system influences a broad range of basic functions from movement to mood.

Aah, mood is what we are interested in! But did you catch that this system also affects movement?

You can now appreciate how a loss of serotonin function can lower the mood and produce depression, as well as lower the level of movement throughout the body. This results in your feeling "down" and at the same time having a loss of energy, increasing sleepiness, weight gain, and sluggishness. In fact, serotonin is only one of dozens of neurotransmitters that all have differing levels of effect. These numerous neurotransmitters work together in a system of checks and balances.

Now Dr. Molly Cule is pointing to a group of musicians waiting in the next room. You may want to cover your ears. It seems the musicians are all playing different songs. The sound is horrible! Dr. Cule saves the day by entering the room, rapping her baton on the podium, and taking control of the orchestra.

Whew! That's much better. Now all of the musicians are playing the same song, at the same tempo, under the direction of our multitalented professor. As Thomas Carew, a Yale researcher, commented, "Serotonin is only one of the molecules of the orchestra. But rather than being the trumpet or cello player, it's the band leader who choreographs the output of the brain."[3]

Let's leave Dr. Molly Cule to her music and continue our exploration of the effects of serotonin. Evidence gained from scientific studies now indicates that low moods—or depression—and low serotonin go together. The normal role of serotonin is to balance and adjust our normal mood shifts. It has a role in "habituation," the process in which the brain learns that a particular recurring sensation is not all that important and should be ignored. It's a little like when you've heard a noise in the

---

Tools for Tomorrow

LifeFilter 16

A "Touch" of God's Love
"'Lord, if you are willing, you can make me clean.' Jesus reached out his hand and touched the man. 'I am willing,' he said. 'Be clean!'" (Luke 5:12b–13a).

Today
1. I will thank God for reaching out and touching me through his Son.
2. I will pass on his love by hugging three people.
3. No matter what my emotions tell me, I will remember that God loves me.

---

background and you've grown used to it. You don't realize it is still there until someone new to your situation points it out. This has happened to me with my children's incessant talking!

When the serotonin system is functioning normally, it helps us keep a steady frame of mind in the face of all of the occurrences around us. It helps us tune out the unimportant stuff and respond in a balanced way to the things that matter.

You can see how the balance of the effects of serotonin in your brain and the effects of your environment work together to determine your mood. Scientific researchers, such as Dr. Molly Cule, who has returned from her orchestra, are discovering much about the chemistry of life and diseases. But do not forget the other half of the equation: your environment, lifestyle, and experiences are just as great an influence. Notice what Dr. Cule is writing on the blackboard: Chemistry + Events = Mood + Behavior.

I hope you can understand the necessity of addressing not only your behavioral patterns and how they enter into this equation, but also the chemistry of your brain. This is why you may need both medication and counseling. The two go hand in hand like the members of an orchestra. Seek to address both sides of the equation, and you may find a new, depression-free balance in your life.

SUMMARY

This is all God asks of you and me: to do what we can. The surprising element in all of this is that when we do what we can with what we have, God blesses in surprising ways. Sometimes, to our astonishment, wonderful things are accomplished.

The next time depression begins infecting you, take your medicine: find someone to hug and touch. You may not believe it at the time, but that touch will eventually help heal you of the numbness that holds you fast.

PHYSICIAN'S FACT

1. Serotonin is the neurotransmitter that "choreographs" the output of the brain.
2. Low serotonin and low mood or depression go together.
3. Chemistry + Events = Mood + Behavior

John L. Mason once said, "The best helping hand you will ever find is at the end of your own arm." Use it to touch others and, in the process, heal yourself.

DAY 17
Depression and Communication

The Power to Win

A persistent cough decided to settle in my chest this past winter. When I wanted to talk, I either constantly kept a cough drop in my mouth, or I hacked and wheezed. As you can imagine, it wasn't a pretty sight. My physician recommended and prescribed several high-powered medicines: steroids, antibiotics, and a variety of cough medicines. One of those was a decongestant. As you probably know, the main function of a decongestant is to thin out—water down, if you will—the thick mucus causing the cough and congestion. As this substance is diluted, the lungs are then better able to expel the invader and breathe more clearly.

Using that analogy, we could say that today's medicine for depression is a decongestant. It dilutes your depression, helping you expel it from your mind and body. If I could use another analogy, I would also call this a "syrup." I don't know about you, but I've never found a cough syrup that tastes good. When I have to take a dose, I hold my nose, grimace, and swallow the stuff. I hate the taste, but I take it anyway because I know it's good for me.

When you are depressed, there is a great temptation to pull yourself into a shell and stay away from everyone. In this dark hole, alone, you concentrate on your problems and magnify your inadequacies. Before long your situation seems so bad, and you feel so unworthy of anything good, that you are pummeled about by the torrent of guilt rushing over you. Bewildered, you sink ever deeper into the black hole your depression has created. Retreating, you become more and more isolated from everyone. You find yourself surrounded by a suffocating, ever-thickening swamp of negativity.

Did I overstate your situation? Probably not. In any case I want to paint as realistic a picture as possible. I want you to see that, left to itself, your depression will grow stronger. As it thickens, this invader clogs the pathways of your emotions and tries to bring all rational thought to a sluggish stop.

> When you are depressed, there is a great temptation to pull yourself into a shell and stay away from everyone.

It's time for the syrup of communication. And, I'm sorry to say, it's a lot like the cough syrups I described earlier. For many of us it won't taste good. Our depression makes us want to stay isolated. It's hard to reach up out of our dark hole and try to communicate with others. But just like the syrup with the bad taste, go ahead and take the medication, no matter how difficult it may be. This is one medicine that works!

An amazing transformation begins to take place when you allow communication with others to enter your life. As you share your thoughts, guilt, and anxieties with others, your depression begins to thin out. Diluted, it is then easier to manage.

Communication, of course, is a two-way street. Both the act of sharing and the act of listening help you gain perspective. Reaching out to someone else forces you out of your hole of isolation. Airing your fears robs them of much of their power. Exposing them to the light of day makes them pale and less significant.

As you prepare to do this, however, I must caution you to be on your guard. Your emotions may well begin screaming at you to stay apart from everyone. Your flight reflex may be on full alert, ready to pull you back from the first hint of meaningful communication. You can overcome this by reminding yourself that depression causes your emotions to paint a false picture. Instead, hold your nose and grimace all you want, but take the "syrup of communication" and begin to get better.

One question that needs to be answered is, with whom should you communicate? First, it is imperative that it be a godly person. In this instance you need someone who is wise, positive, encouraging, and who cares about you. It may be a close friend; in my life, my wife fills this role wonderfully. It might also be a Christian counselor or a church staff member who is gifted in this area. Above all, don't stay isolated.

Finally, make sure you communicate with God. As you reach out of your isolation to him, you will find a nail-scarred hand already reaching out toward you to give understanding, love, and strength.

Perhaps the words of David express how you feel: "Listen to my prayer, O God, do not ignore my plea; hear me and answer me. My thoughts trouble me and I am distraught" (Ps. 55:1–2).

Do you feel like this? Evidently, you're not alone. David was Israel's greatest king and the composer of more psalms than any other person, but even he had times of emotional difficulty. As the psalm suggests, however, David did not stay isolated. Instead, he poured out his heart to God. In doing so, he learned an important lesson—and he has passed it on to you: "Trust in him at all times, O people; pour out your hearts to him, for God is our refuge" (Ps. 62:8).

God is your refuge. He wants to listen to you. Communicate with him today and with those around you as well. As you do, you'll find your depression diluted, your mood lifted, and your emotions strengthened.

STRENGTH FOR TODAY
Eye of Newt and Wort of Frog

I examined the elderly woman and noted her extreme pallor and shortness of breath. She lay on the stretcher in the emergency room in a listless, unresponsive stupor. When I had entered the room earlier, her daughter had stepped back from the stretcher, an object cradled carefully in her hands. After examining the elderly woman and dispatching a nurse for appropriate therapy, I turned my attention to the daughter. I wanted to see what she was holding that was so precious. It was a small bottle of turpentine. She explained that when her mother would get short of breath, inhaling the turpentine cleared up her lungs.

Skeptically, I nodded and noticed a canvas bag containing two quart jars sitting in the corner. When I pointed them out, the daughter withdrew one jar containing a thick, white paste. She said she had looked all day in the woods for a perfect hillside of white clay. Whenever her mother became weak, she would eat bowls of the white clay to cleanse her bowels! The daughter winked as she shared that only she knew where to find this precious bank of white clay but would be glad to share it with me if I helped her grandmother get better.

At this point my anger was growing, and I really wasn't ready for the final development. The last jar contained a thick, ruddy suspension of red particles, and to my amazement I could make out dozens of rusty nails swirling in the fluid. The daughter was most proud of this jar. It contained "iron water" to help her mother's blood.

Over the years I have encountered treatments and therapies even more bizarre than the white clay and iron water. Folk remedies from the countryside now vie for attention with New Age treatments from the Far East. Step into any drugstore and take a look at all the alternative medications from ginseng to palmetto saw grass. What should you do? Are these therapies truly effective? How do you avoid getting "snookered"? Let me discuss some of the more common non-medication therapies for depression, and we'll get to the root of the problem.

Wort is an Old English word for "plant." St. John refers to John the Baptist, whose birthday supposedly falls on June 24, in or around the time this plant produces its yellow flowers—thus, the name St. John's Wort (*Hypericum perforatum*). Traditionally this flower has been used for years for wound healing. Does it really work? German scientists discovered this plant contains a monoamine oxidase inhibitor, one of the classes of antidepressant medications. Recent studies from 1996 verify the relief from depression was similar to that experienced from pharmaceutical antidepressants. The negative side of using this plant is the erratic dosage, the cross-reaction of MAO inhibitors with certain types of food, and the fact that MAO inhibitors are some of the oldest classes of antidepressants and have been replaced by much more effective treatments.

European researchers recruited forty elderly individuals with depression and poor blood flow to their brain and gave them eighty milligrams of ginkgo (*Ginkgo biloba*) extract three times a day. The good news: their depression lifted, and their mental facilities improved significantly. The bad news: unfortunately, they suffered from diarrhea, restlessness, and irritability.

Drink a cola or a cup of coffee, and you have taken in the nation's most popular "pick me up," caffeine. Caffeine has a mild but noticeable antidepressant effect as well as its ability to "wake you up." However, if you've ever had one cup of coffee too much, you are familiar with the side effects of insomnia, agitation, restlessness, and irritability.

A minor vitamin B6 deficiency can reduce the availability of brain chemicals such as serotonin. Several studies have shown that depressed individuals tend to have low blood levels of this nutrient. As little as ten milligrams of B6 a day can help combat depression. In addition, vitamins B1, B2, and folic acid also prove advantageous in combating depression. So, by all means, take your vitamins!

Recent studies in brain chemistry have shown that taking natural substances used in the production of serotonin may alter levels of brain chemistry and reverse depression. Two such substances are gaining popularity, Tryptophan and 5-Hydroxyl L-Tryptophan (5-HTP). Studies indicate these serotonin "precursors," or ingredients necessary for the production of serotonin, increase levels of the "feel good" hormones of the brain, endorphins. These endorphins benefit patients with severe depression. However, in the study, the substance had to be taken at a different time of the day than antidepressant medications were taken.

What is the bottom line? All of these substances work in ways similar to antidepressant medications. In fact, if you are taking medication, the two substances will interact and can produce disastrous results. So

---

Tools for Tomorrow

LifeFilter 17

Using Communication as a Cure

"Trust in him at all times . . . pour out your hearts to him, for God is our refuge" (Ps. 62:8).

Today

1. I will communicate with God and believe that he hears me.

2. I will open lines of communication through meaningful dialogue with others.

3. I will communicate with my soul by reading and meditating on God's Word.

what should you do? Talk to your physician. Don't rely completely on an alternative medication. You may be courting disaster.

In my humble opinion these alternative therapies, while having some basis for effectiveness, have more of a positive effect because of their "placebo" effect. A placebo is a "sugar" pill or a replacement medication that contains no active ingredients. It is given in medical trials to see if the trial medication has a different effect than the placebo. However, scientists have discovered that patients can benefit from the expectation of positive results and actually get better.

In the case of depression, this benefit comes from taking an active role in intervening in your depression. By taking an alternative therapy, you are taking a positive step toward conquering depression. Just deciding to do something about your depression will benefit you. Some, if not most, of the benefit from an alternative medication may be this placebo effect. Don't knock it, though. Any help is good help. Just make sure that whatever medication or alternative medication you take is approved by your physician.

SUMMARY

PHYSICIAN'S FACT

1. Some herbal remedies have merit because they contain ingredients found in traditional antidepressant medications.

2. Taking vitamins has proven to be a helpful addition to antidepressant treatment.

3. The positive effect of alternative therapies may have as much to do with taking an active role in your treatment as the inherent benefits of the substance.

Our depression makes us want to stay isolated. It's hard to reach up out of our dark hole and try to communicate with others. But just like the syrup with the bad taste, go ahead and take the syrup of communication, no matter how difficult it may be. This is one medicine that works!

An amazing transformation begins to take place when you allow communication with others to enter your life. As you share your thoughts, guilt, and anxieties with others, your depression begins to thin out. Diluted, it is then easier to manage.

Part 4

Small Weapons That Win a Big Victory

We are well over halfway through the thirty-day plan for helping you conquer your depression. If you've stayed with us this far, Bruce and I want to congratulate you! You have probably learned more about the nature and effects of depression. As you have seen its physical causes and as you have begun to learn how to counter its effects in your life, we hope you are learning this lesson: It is possible to live with depression and not succumb to it!

- We have shown you what depression is so that you no longer have to fear it.
- We have taught you how to embrace depression when it appears and use it to become closer to God.
- We have provided you with tools that can lessen depression's hold upon you.
- We have given you medicine to take that will make you stronger and help you to feel better.

Your inventory of helps for getting over depression is now impressive. Bruce and I, however, are part of your team, and we believe you can become even stronger. We want to shrink depression in your eyes until it is no longer a giant bully pushing you around any way it wants.

Remember Goliath? He was big, and he was a bully. David, facing him, was small, and the enemy laughed at him. But when the smoke cleared, the bully was dead on the ground, and David was still on his feet. What made the difference for David? He trusted in God, and he had the right weapons.

> What made the difference for David? He trusted in God, and he had the right weapons.

For the next several days, we are going to give you an arsenal of weapons with which you can defeat depression when it comes to bully you. Your firepower is getting ready to grow. You will now be able to go on the offensive. So get your sling ready! No matter how big and strong you believe your depression to be, begin to think of yourself as David.

DAY 18
Using the Weapon That Depresses Depression

THE POWER TO WIN

Did you ever have a boxing clown? At some point in my boyhood, I got one for a birthday present. This inflatable toy had a round bottom and was painted to look like a clown. The idea was to hit it as often as you wanted. Maybe it was supposed to help you learn to box; if so, I was a miserable failure. In any case, this opponent was a pushover—literally. It never tried to fight back, never defended itself, never got mad at me. Always smiling and standing still, it presented a beautiful target I could pummel to my heart's content. But a funny thing happened with the boxing clown. I lost every fight I had with it.

I was the one doing the punching and the knocking down. I was the one who should have won. But the clown had a secret. Because of its round bottom, it never stayed knocked over. No matter how many times I punched the clown's lights out, it always came back upright. By the end of the fight, I was exhausted. Punched out and worn out, I was ready to quit. But my opponent, the clown, still stood there, smiling that infuriating grin at me. When I left the room, I sometimes imagined it raising its arms in victory behind my back—smiling all the while, of course.

Perseverance. After faith, it's the strongest weapon we have with which to fight depression. It helps us break a deadly cycle of which we may not even be aware. And breaking that cycle produces some positive side effects: new, powerful habits that actually act as our allies.

How does the weapon of perseverance accomplish all this? First, let's take a look at this deadly cycle.

When we notice depression's arrival, what is our reaction? In my counseling and discussions with depressed people, I've discovered we initially react in one of two ways. Some of us are always caught by surprise. We never expect the depression to return again and can't see it coming until it has completely surrounded us. Others of us know our depression is pretty regular; we understand its signs and can watch as it approaches and settles in.

That is the first stage of the cycle of depression. But whether we are surprised by its appearance or we see it coming, we often react in the same way to the cycle's second stage, and this is the part that is most important—and deadly.

Let me talk directly to you for a moment. After realizing you are experiencing a depressive episode, how do you react? If you are like many I've counseled, you give up. You throw up your hands and say, "Depression is here again. There's nothing I can do about it." And then you let the disease dictate how you will react emotionally. Black moods and periods of doubt control you until the depression leaves and the cycle, for the moment, is complete. Then you wait, without realizing it, for the next cycle to begin.

But what if you changed the cycle? Believe it or not, it is within your power to do so. Again, you may not be able to stop depression from descending on you, but you can choose how you will respond to it. I don't know how many times I've already stated this in these pages, but I want to pound this into your thinking.

Here's where the weapon of perseverance delivers a mortal blow to your enemy. You simply tell depression: "I'm never giving up or giving in to you. You may continue to plague me, but I'll fight you with everything I've got. My emotions don't belong to you, and I refuse to let them be held hostage without a fight. You may knock me down, but I've decided to keep on getting up. And I'll fight you every time."

What does this type of attitude accomplish?

- It breaks your usual cycle. You no longer simply give up when depression hits you.
- The process of deciding to fight depression, _even when you don't feel like doing so,_ begins to give you more control over your emotions and helps you no longer feel like a victim.
- As you decide to fight depression every time it appears, you build confidence in yourself. In many cases this shortens the amount of time depression stays with you.
- Using the weapon of perseverance on a regular basis builds powerful habits in your behavior. Use it long enough and eventually you begin fighting depression when it appears without even realizing it!

Let me give you a word of encouragement. Even a little effort on your part each time is helpful. Even if you can't successfully fight off depression this time, but begin trying to do so, you have made progress. Making the decision to do what you can each time will make you stronger. Perseverance pays off.

Flash back to 1968. The Mexico City Olympics are taking place amid great fanfare. As the marathon contestants line up, spectators buzz about possible winners of the race that gave birth to the entire Olympic movement. Most of the attention focuses on Mamo Wolde of Ethiopia, and rightly so; he will win the marathon. But he will not be the only winner that day.

With the crack of the starter's gun, the contestants begin their quest for a gold medal. One of the runners, John Stephen Akhwari of Tanzania, finds himself trapped in the middle of some other runners several miles into the race. Unable to see well, he falls and hurts his leg horribly. He watches in anguish as the other racers continue. The marathon will not be won by John Stephen Akhwari on this day. He has come to Mexico City and failed . . . or has he?

Now flash forward to the end of the race. Wolde, the Ethiopian, has already won. An hour has passed, darkness is falling, and the last spectators are leaving the stadium. Suddenly their attention is drawn to the sounds of police sirens. The marathon gate to the stadium is thrown open, and, unbelievably, a lone runner stumbles into the stadium for his last lap. It is John Stephen Akhwari. Hobbling painfully on his bandaged leg, grimacing with every step, knowing he cannot win the race, he continues all the same. Finally he crosses the finish line and collapses.

Why, someone asked him, didn't he stop after injuring himself? After all, there was no way he could win the race. Listen to John Stephen Akhwari's response: "My country did not send me to Mexico City to start the race," he said with dignity. "They sent me to finish the race."[1]

Perseverance is a powerful weapon.

Let's flash back two thousand years to another man who knew how to persevere. The apostle Paul was a man who devoted himself wholly, unselfishly, to God. But it certainly did not ensure him a life of pleasure and ease. You could say his life was maxed out with beatings, persecutions, and, to add insult to injury, multiple imprisonments. These prisons, I might add, had no weight rooms, color television, or time off for good behavior. In addition, some of Paul's peers criticized the apostle for getting himself into what they believed were embarrassing circumstances.

Paul, put in prison once more, could have given up. Instead, he had this to say: "I am not ashamed, because I know whom I have believed, and am convinced that he is able to guard what I have entrusted to him for that day" (2 Tim. 1:12). Paul knew God would not fail him. He believed that the Christian who stayed faithful, even in the tough times, would be ultimately blessed for his perseverance.

God has a special place in his heart for those who endure. Human power doesn't interest him. Dynamic personalities and great people skills don't impress him. He sees through smiles and designer clothes, looking for something more. "The eyes of the LORD are on those who fear him, on those whose hope is in his unfailing love" (Ps. 33:18). If you're giving the best of yourself to God and trusting in Christ to save you, then the heavenly Father's eyes are on you. He blesses you every time you get knocked down by depression and then get up, still trusting God and still willing to live for him. Looked at in this way, depression does not make you a failure. Instead, it makes you a strong Christian and a winner in God's eyes.

Even if depression keeps knocking you down, make the decision today to keep getting up. Let Paul's creed also be yours: "Therefore put on the full armor of God, so that when the day of evil comes, you may be able to stand your ground, and after you have done everything, to stand" (Eph. 6:13).

Keep on standing.

STRENGTH FOR TODAY
Of Magnets, Massage, and Music

Gary was once a nuclear engineer on one of the Navy's finest nuclear submarines. During the eighties, when the Soviet Union was still a threat to America, he was the man who had the responsibility of turning the last key to launch the war to end all wars. Since then, Gary has become an engineer in the department of radiology at the hospital where I have my office. He is an intelligent man. He is a highly educated man. He is a man of science.

Having come from such a highly technical background, I was somewhat taken aback when I saw him walking down the hall with something shiny on his earlobes. At first, I suspected he had donned a pair of earrings. When I stopped him and inspected his ears more closely, however, I discovered he had placed an ordinary staple through the bottom of each lobe. I asked him if he had an encounter with a deranged electric staple gun, and he laughed. But the truth was even more bizarre. According to him, putting a staple through the earlobe was the latest way to stop smoking. Just tug on a staple each time you wanted a cigarette, and the craving would vanish. When I asked him the source of this new treatment, he quoted a recently published article from one of those tabloids found in the checkout line at grocery stores.

As P. T. Barnum said, a sucker is born every minute. In spite of his high intelligence and the fact he once protected our freedom from Communism, this engineer was willing to staple his earlobes to stop smoking!

We have discussed traditional medical therapy and alternative medical therapy. But other forms of therapy are equally as bizarre sounding as the aforementioned treatment.

At Mie University in Tsu, Japan, psychiatrists studied twelve men hospitalized for serious depression and already on medication. The researchers exposed them to a strong citrus fragrance. Amazingly, after eleven weeks all medication requirements had decreased significantly. After several months they were able to stop taking medication altogether. Aromatherapy is a growing trend in America that has been adopted from these types of studies in the Far East. Its true efficacy is yet to be proved. But you smell good!

In the Bible, King Saul showed classic signs of depression and asked the future king, David, to play music for him. In a recent study, people suffering from serious depression received either weekly visits from a music therapist, taped music to play on their own, or no music. Compared to the control group, participants in both music groups showed significantly improved moods.

At the University of Arizona, John J. Allen, an assistant professor of psychology, studied thirty-four women suffering from major depression and on no medication. One-third met with the researchers but received no acupuncture. The second group received acupuncture but not on "points" recommended for treating depression. The third group received acupuncture on the depression points. Compared to the two control groups, the women receiving acupuncture on the depression points showed significantly greater relief from depression.

In the Touch Research Institute at the University of Miami Medical School in Florida, psychologist Tiffany Field had massage therapists give twenty-minute Swedish massages twice a week to women suffering from serious postpartum depression. They reported improved mood and relief of depression. This confirms that touch is the only sense human beings cannot live without.

Tools for Tomorrow

LifeFilter 18

Keep on Standing

"Therefore put on the full armor of God, so that when the day of evil comes, you may be able to stand your ground, and after you have done everything, to stand" (Eph. 6:13).

Today

1. I will rest in the fact that God will *never* give up on me.
2. I resolve to fight my depression and not give up!
3. I will remember God has a special place in his heart for those who endure.

A study under way at the University of Pennsylvania is comparing traditional electro-convulsive therapy (ECT or shock therapy) with a new therapy, transcranial magnetic stimulation (TMS). TMS delivers a mild magnetic pulse that jump-starts the part of the brain responsible for severe depression. While ECT requires general anaesthesia and shocks to the brain that can induce seizures, TMS is much less involved. Patients are treated in an outpatient exam room while sitting in a comfortable recliner. They are awake, alert, and require no medication. So far, patients have responded well to TMS treatments over a one- to two-week period. Results are still pending, but this form of treatment for the more severe forms of depression may be helpful in the future.

So take your pick. Try listening to some relaxing music while sniffing an orange and receiving a massage from an acupuncturist! These treatments we've just discussed all contribute to the treatment of depression. In fact, massage therapy and music therapy reinforce some of the principles we have already discussed regarding having more fun and making touch a part of your life. But with the exception of TMS, these alternative therapies are only adjuncts to conventional therapy and should not be considered replacements.

SUMMARY

Here's where the weapon of perseverance delivers a mortal blow to your enemy. Simply tell depression: "I'm never giving up or giving in to you. You may continue to plague me, but I'll fight you with everything I've got. My emotions don't belong to you, and I refuse to let them be held hostage without a fight. You may knock me down, but I've decided to keep on getting up. And I'll fight you every time."

What does this type of attitude accomplish?

- It breaks your usual cycle. You no longer simply give up when depression hits you.
- The process of deciding to fight depression, _even when you don't feel like doing so,_ begins to give you more control over your emotions and helps you no longer feel like a victim.

- As you decide to fight depression every time it appears, you build confidence in yourself. In many cases this shortens the amount of time depression stays with you.
- Using the weapon of perseverance on a regular basis builds powerful habits in your behavior. Use it long enough and eventually you begin fighting depression when it appears without even realizing it!

PHYSICIAN'S FACT

1. Alternative nonmedical methods of treatment for depression may help you get better but should not replace conventional therapy.

2. TMS may prove to be a new avenue of treatment for difficult cases of depression.

3. Alternative therapies work best when they reinforce already established areas of need.

DAY 19
Learning to Say No to Inappropriate Requests

THE POWER TO WIN

A short, portly, middle-aged business executive named John started to walk into heaven but found St. Peter blocking his way. "Just a minute," the saint said as he opened a large book. After flipping through its pages, he looked up. "Sorry, your name's not in here. You can't come in."

"But that's impossible," John protested. Then he had a thought. "How often is this book updated?"

"Every fifteen minutes," came the reply.

John smiled. "Then that explains it. I've only just died. If we wait a few minutes, I'm sure you'll find my name appearing."

"We can do that," St. Peter agreed. "But while we're waiting, we might as well use the time constructively. I need to know if you've ever done anything wonderful or brave during your life."

"As a matter of fact, I've done something that I believe would qualify as both," John said, a note of pride creeping into his voice. "I once saw a fierce gang of bikers trying to mug an elderly woman. I looked around and saw there was no one to help me, but I felt I had to do something anyway. So I grabbed the leader by the arm, spun him around to face me, and told him to stop or else."

St. Peter was impressed. "When did you do this?" he asked.

"About five minutes ago," John admitted.

Have you ever found yourself in a situation where you felt there was no way out? Someone is asking you to do something inappropriate, but you can't find it in your heart to say no, even if, like John in the above story, you know it may cause you much harm. Because you don't want anyone to be mad at you or disappointed, you swallow hard and say, "Yes, I'll do it." In the process your self-image plummets and your depression deepens. The worst thing is, if someone makes another inappropriate request, you'll acquiesce again and again and again.

Inappropriate requests can cover a multitude of situations.

- You are bone tired and need rest. The person who is asking you to do something either has the time to do it or can ask someone else. Will you do it anyway?
- You have worked hard to get your part of a project done. A coworker who has not done her part now asks you for help at the last instant. Will you rescue her?
- An acquaintance who is not good with money asks you for a loan or, worse, a gift. You know he has wasted money or he has not worked at a job when he could. Will you give in to him anyway?

In other words, in all of the above situations, will you let others use you?

Think about your self-image for a moment. Are you so dependent on the approval of others that you must ignore what your conscience or body tells you and give in to unreasonable requests? After all, your friends certainly don't have a problem saying no. You hear them say it all the time—probably to you. So why can't you do the same thing?

If you think it's wrong to say no, then let me set you straight. God has given you a brain and the ability to use it. He has promised to place his Spirit in your life to help you know what is right and what is wrong. Maybe you don't want to say no and hurt someone's feelings. But think about this for a moment: When you respond positively to inappropriate requests, you are actually saying no to God's Spirit within you and denying the quality of the intelligence he gave you!

Jesus never let the expectations of others determine his actions. Take, for example, an incident at the beginning of his earthly ministry.

He had begun speaking and healing in the region of Galilee. Because of their willingness to believe, the people saw mighty miracles when they brought the blind, lame, and deaf to Jesus. The message quickly spread throughout the area that a wonderful miracle worker was in their midst. It culminated in the following incident: "That evening after sunset the people brought to Jesus all the sick and demon-possessed. The whole town gathered at the door, and Jesus healed many who had various diseases" (Mark 1:32–34a).

> When you respond positively to inappropriate requests, you are actually saying no to God's Spirit within you and denying the quality of the intelligence he gave you!

Now the next day has dawned. Excitement among the people has risen to a fever pitch as they make their way toward the house where Jesus is staying. The crowds swell. Perhaps merchants set up their booths in anticipation of a busy day with a hungry crowd. Adrenaline flows strong in the veins of the disciples. They talk excitedly among themselves about the future of Jesus and their place in that future. As the popularity of their Master grows, they will be a part of it!

The noise of the crowd around the house where Jesus and his followers have spent the night is now so loud that conversation is impossible. The knocks begin; the people are excited; the needs are urgent.

If you were Christ, what would you do?

The verses following those we've just read give us a brief but startling response by the Son of God: "Very early in the morning, while it was still dark, Jesus got up, left the house and went off to a solitary place, where he prayed. Simon and his companions went to look for him, and when they found him, they exclaimed: 'Everyone is looking for you!'

"Jesus replied, 'Let us go somewhere else—to the nearby villages—so I can preach there also. That is why I have come'" (Mark 1:35–38).

What was Jesus thinking? People at the house were waiting to be healed. Steadily gathering crowds were eagerly anticipating a glimpse of him so they could give him adulation. The world, at least in Galilee, was his for the taking. But Jesus didn't let others' agendas determine what he knew was wrong and right.

Let's take a moment to examine why Jesus acted as he did:

- He knew the importance of spiritual refreshment. Regular, un-interrupted time with God was so important to him that it superceded everything else.
- He knew that filling others' needs was no substitute for doing God's will in his own life.
- Jesus refused to let anyone's definition of urgent take the place of what he knew was right for himself. (Please read that sentence again!)

We can learn some important principles for our own life by looking at Christ's life.

If anyone ever loved others, Jesus did. He had not only created everyone with whom he came in contact, but he also knew that one day he would die for them! But that did not keep him from saying no to their requests from time to time. In fact, sometimes saying no can be one of the most loving things you do! True love does not repeatedly rescue someone from the consequences of bad behavior. This only enables the person to continue a sinful lifestyle and makes you feel used. True love forgives, but it also encourages positive change by allowing the persons to discover why they need to change and move toward God and his will.

Remember this incident from the life of Jesus the next time someone asks you to do something you believe would not be good. If you say no, several things will happen. First, to your astonishment, the world will not stop. Second, the person asking will still be your friend (if he breaks off the relationship because of this, there was no friendship to begin with; it was only a user relationship for him). Third, your self-esteem will begin going up as you are true to what you believe to be right—and better self-esteem means a happier person. Finally, a rise in self-esteem makes you better able to fight off the effects of depression.

One other note before leaving this topic. One of the wisest people I know regularly says no to many people. He is still well liked and respected greatly by those who know him. If the truth be known, much of his respect is earned by his ability to say no to inappropriate requests. Having this weapon in his spiritual and emotional arsenal has been a powerful boost to his life.

What Jesus did, and what this wise friend does, can also be a part of your own life. Take the weapon of "no" and use it to fight off inappropriate requests. You'll discover that, after a time, the number of these types of requests will begin to fall off. You'll see people's respect for you grow. And you will, yourself, discover that using this powerful weapon has made you stronger and depression weaker.

STRENGTH FOR TODAY
Bipolar or Unipolar?

The different ways depression manifests itself cannot be lumped together into one category. In fact, there are many types of depression and several specialized forms of depression.

Bipolar Depression

My friend's face was weary in spite of his smile.

"Guess what my wife did yesterday while I was at work?" he asked. "She bought a house on the lake."

I frowned. "I didn't know you were planning to move."

"We weren't. She went down to the lake, saw a For Sale sign, and told the man she would pay him whatever he wanted. We sign the contract next week."

Alarm bells were going off in my head. He had told me similar tales for weeks now, his wife purchasing increasingly expensive items. But a house? I saw the symptoms. She was in the manic phase of manic-depressive disorder. But after gently expressing my opinion, I listened in sorrow as my friend denied his wife was having any problems. Two weeks later she was committed to a behavioral institute for psychotic manifestations of manic-depressive disorder.

Bipolar depression, or manic-depressive disorder, is far too complex to discuss in this book. However, you should be aware of the dual nature of this unusual disease. Patients suffer from soaring highs and blistering lows. One day they can be on top of the world, invincible and able to do anything. The next day they may be paralyzed by deep, dark depression.

While in the manic phase, people believe they are invincible and all-powerful. They get little sleep, spend money they don't have, and make unrealistic plans for the future. But after days and weeks of feeling this way, they plummet back to earth, only to see what they believe is a dark and dreary world.

As in major depression, bipolar disorder results from imbalance of brain chemistry. Recognizing bipolar disorder is important, for the patient will require medication. In addition, the type of treatment is different from the treatment for conventional depression.

Unipolar Depression

Unipolar depression is another term for clinical depression without a manic component. This term refers to the type of depression many people call "normal" depression. Much of this book is devoted to treating and alleviating unipolar depression, though persons suffering from other types of depression can also benefit.

Depression in Adolescence

As I write these words, another high school shooting has occurred. With alarming frequency such violence by teenagers against teenagers is increasing. Today's teens see more of what life is all about—good and evil—than ever before. Television, movies, video games, and the Internet bombard them with the harsh reality of this existence, and the even harsher virtual reality of their imagination. With the prevalence of drugs, AIDS, and teen violence, it is no wonder today's teenagers have a high incidence of depression.

The incidence of suicide in teenagers has tripled since 1960, and it is the third-leading cause of death in adolescents. Warning signs include:

- Poor performance in school.
- Withdrawal from friends and activities.
- Sadness and hopelessness.
- Lack of energy.
- Anger and rage.
- Poor self-esteem.
- Substance abuse.
- Suicidal thoughts.

Teenagers suffering from depression need prompt, professional treatment. Depression in teenagers can rapidly progress to a life-threatening stage. If you are a teenager who is depressed, or if you suspect a teenager is depressed, don't delay. Get help now!

Depression in Later Life

My grandmother died when I was thirteen. I remember the loss clearly. But I remember my grandfather's last years with greater clarity. We buried my grandmother in the cemetery beside the tiny church she had attended for all of her seventy-eight years. Their home sat just across the street from the church. My grandfather seemed to lose interest in his garden about that time. Instead of plowing his ten acres behind his old mule, he would sit for hours on his screened-in back porch, my grandmother's tombstone clearly visible across the street. In time his health went steadily down. Seven years later he went on to join his wife in heaven.

I watched my grandfather descend into the depression of the elderly. Unfortunately, his generation never learned the real meaning of depression. And thirty years ago physicians failed to realize the medical impact of depression in senior adults.

> ## Tools for Tomorrow
>
> ### LIFEFILTER 19
>
> _Know the Power of "No!"_
> "If any of you lacks wisdom, he should ask God, who gives generously to all without finding fault, and it will be given to him" (James 1:5).
>
> ### TODAY
>
> 1. Remember that filling others' needs is not a substitute for doing God's will in my life.
> 2. I will say no to requests I believe are inappropriate.
> 3. Now that I know the different types of depression, I will examine my emotions to see if they are being influenced by this disease.

The fact is that women who turn fifty and don't have cancer or heart disease can often live another forty years. Men who make it to sixty-five in good health can often expect to turn eighty-one. With the right kind of preventive caution and medical recognition of depression, the elderly should have no reason not to enjoy the golden years of their life.

There is, however, a weed in this wonderful garden of long life. Fifteen out of every one hundred adults over the age of sixty-five suffer from depression. When depression occurs late in life, it is often debilitating, interfering with the ability to function normally. Recognizing this type of depression can be difficult. Today's senior adults grew up in a time when depression was not understood to be a biological disorder. Therefore, they are less willing to recognize their own problems. Sometimes the elderly are labeled with a frivolous diagnosis such as "senility" or "being contrary."

Most of the time, depression is due to an underlying chronic illness or confinement to the hospital or a nursing home. Untreated depression can lead to disability, worsening of the symptoms of other illnesses, premature death, and suicide. The good news is that with proper diagnosis, 80 percent of depressed senior adults recover and return to a normal life.

Most importantly, recognition of a long life span while you are under the age of fifty should encourage you to plan ahead. Exercise and eat healthily. Establish a good support network of friends and family. Be realistic about your abilities, and maintain an active lifestyle. By doing these things, you will help stave off the threat of depression during your senior years.

SUMMARY

If you think it's wrong to say no, then let me set you straight. God has given you a brain and the ability to use it. He has promised to place his Spirit in your life to help you know what is right and what is wrong. Maybe you don't want to say no and hurt someone's feelings. But think about this for a moment: When you respond positively to inappropriate requests, you are actually saying no to God's Spirit within you and denying the quality of the intelligence he gave you!

Instead, take the weapon of "no!" and use it to fight off inappropriate requests.

> ### PHYSICIAN'S FACT
>
> 1. Bipolar disorder includes periods of unusual highs and terrible lows.
> 2. Depression can be deadly in teenagers and should be recognized promptly.
> 3. Depression in the elderly is not a normal part of life and can be successfully treated.

You'll discover that after a time the number of these types of requests will begin to diminish. You'll see people's respect for you grow. And you will discover that using this powerful weapon has made you stronger and depression weaker.

DAY 20
Hitting the Target with Goals

THE POWER TO WIN

General Sedgwick, who commanded troops for the North in the Civil War, is known today chiefly because of his last words. His forces were waging a fierce battle with one of the Southern armies. Bullets and cannonballs began to fly, some of them dangerously close to the general. Unperturbed, he continued to sit atop his horse, surveying the battle scene before him. When several aids advised him it would be prudent for him to move back a bit, the general made history. Snorting derisively at the suggestion, he said, "Why, those gunners couldn't hit an elephant at this dist—"

How accurate are you with the weapons we've given you over the past several days? What can you hit with them?

Today we're going to add the weapon of setting goals to your increasingly powerful arsenal. This weapon not only gives you another way to defeat depression, but it also:

- makes your tools work efficiently;
- strengthens the medicines you take, making them more effective; and
- helps you fire your other weapons more accurately.

Setting goals helps you know you're making progress. It also shows the path your life is taking. Think of goals as stepping-stones: each one not only helps you get across a difficult stream, but it also shows where you've been. If the stones are too far apart, you'll miss the next jump and fall into the water. If you quit putting down the stones, you'll be stranded in the middle of the stream, unable to continue.

I'm amazed at the number of people who come into my office for counseling who seem, to the casual observer, to be successful people. A careful look beneath the surface, however, often reveals they are floundering. As I ask them what they want from life, they may be able to articulate several goals: happiness, wealth, a good marriage. But when I ask them what they are doing to ensure reaching their goals, they usually give me a blank look. Nor can they understand why the goals they've set are still unattainable. The problem is that their goals, while worthwhile, are too far from where they are presently. The stones are too far apart.

Remember the old story about the new Baptist minister in town? He was invited by the Methodist preacher and the Catholic priest to go fishing with them. Wanting to show his spirit of cooperation, and having a great love of fishing, he accepted.

When the three got to the local lake, they rowed to its center and began fishing. A few moments later the priest said, "I forgot my favorite lure." Then, to the astonishment of the Baptist pastor, he got out of the boat and began walking across the water! All the way to the bank and back to the boat, the Baptist saw this Catholic priest doing what he had only read about in the Bible.

About an hour later the Methodist said, "I'm hungry. Think I'll go back to the car and get a couple of sandwiches for us." And following the priest's example, he also stepped out of the boat in the middle of the lake and walked across the water to the car and then back again.

By this time the Baptist's eyes were as big as saucers. He was thinking to himself, *I've got as much faith as these guys. If they can walk on water, so can I.*

He worked on his courage for awhile and finally said casually, "Listen, guys, I forgot something. I'll be right back." And, stepping out of the boat, he went straight to the bottom! As he sputtered and coughed his way back to the boat, the priest looked at the Methodist and said, "Think we should show him where the stones are?"

It's important to know where the stones are in your life. For example, did you know you're putting down stones at this moment? Whether you realize it or not, the process of reading this book each day causes you to set—and reach—small goals. Look back through this book. Nineteen firm stones form a path that leads you away from hopeless depression and toward a healthy emotional life. That's nineteen goals you've set and reached. Each goal is not only a stepping-stone, but it also becomes a part of the firepower in your arsenal, making you even more powerful and accurate.

What other goals can you set and try to reach? Before you begin trying to set some, remember not to set them too far from where you are—unless you can put down smaller, closer goals that allow you to reach your ultimate destination. For example, you might set this goal: "I want to conquer my depression." That's a great goal! If you could get there, you'd have a weapon that would blast depression to smithereens. But how do you get there? That's where some smaller daily and weekly goals become necessary. Let's look at some possibilities:

1. I will learn more about what causes depression.
2. I will read one chapter in this book each day and try to apply it to my life.
3. I will find a physician with whom I am comfortable and allow him/her to help me with my depression.
4. I will pray to God every day, regardless of my emotional state.

You could add many more to these four; this is only a beginning suggestion. Let the list be as long as you wish. The important thing is for these goals to be attainable and to lead you in the right direction.

Take a moment to reflect honestly on your life. What ultimate goals would you like to set? Now, what smaller goals do you need to place in front of you to build a path that will lead you to that ultimate goal?

Be careful. You must avoid falling into the trap of saying something like this: "I've tried some of this before and it never has worked. Why should it work now?" This kind of reasoning is always wrong! That's because it presupposes you can never change. Just because you failed in the past doesn't mean you'll fail now. After all, you've grown wiser and more knowledgeable over the past several years. You also have more tools, like this book and a growing faith in God, to help you succeed.

And always remember: As a Christian, your future will always be brighter than your past.

In the New Testament, Paul gives us an excellent example of how to set and meet goals regardless of what has happened in the past. "I want to know Christ and the power of his resurrection and the fellowship of sharing in his sufferings, becoming like him in his death, and so, somehow, to attain to the resurrection from the dead" (Phil. 3:10–11). In these two verses Paul sets his ultimate goals. Then he admits he hasn't reached all of them yet: "Not that I have already obtained all this, or have already been made perfect" (Phil. 3:12a). But is this great man discouraged because he hasn't yet completed all these worthy goals? Not at all! Instead he tells the reader he intends to keep on putting down stones, to keep on adding weapons to his arsenal, as he moves forward in his life: "But one thing I do: Forgetting what is behind and straining toward what is ahead, I press on toward the goal to win the prize for which God has called me heavenward in Christ Jesus" (Phil. 3:13–14).

Did Paul ever fail? Certainly. Sometimes he failed spectacularly. Did this stop him? No! Look again at these words. Paul uses strong images like "strain" and "press." The apostle is making a deliberate effort to move in a forward direction toward Christ and away from a hurtful past.

Paul was a powerful Christian. You can be like him. Use the weapon of setting goals to focus accurately on overcoming depression and moving forward toward a healthy, joyous life.

Place your stones carefully. Set your goals wisely. And press on.

Strength for Today
Sleep and Energy

I gazed into the mirror at the creature staring back at me. His hair stood on end. His eyes were bloodshot. His face was worn and haggard.

I had spent four days on call as an intern at the hospital. In four nights I had taken only a thirty-minute nap. When I had arrived at home with the prospect of two days of rest, I knew I would collapse into my bed. I felt like I could sleep for forty-eight hours!

Now, twelve hours after coming home, I was wide awake. How could I still be functioning with so little sleep? I had to sleep. Now! But sleep would not come. My mind felt like soft jelly, sloshing around in my skull. I couldn't think. I couldn't concentrate. My vision was blurred. I needed sleep.

Have you ever felt like this? Your mind seems on fire, whirling at a dizzying pace and yet unable to focus on a single coherent thought? Or perhaps you have had the opposite experience. By 7:00 P.M. you are so sleepy you can barely make it to the bed. You pour yourself under the covers and sleep for twelve hours. When you awaken, you feel tired and lethargic and can barely drag yourself out of the bed. Nothing seems to wake you or give you energy.

A few years back, when I fell into deep depression, all I wanted to do was stay in the bed and sleep. And yet, in spite of hours of sleep, I could find no energy.

Just what is going on inside your brain to cause this drastic alteration in sleep?

Let us journey deep within the substance of your brain. We have already traveled into the netherworld of your mind once; now we return to the center of your brain. Nestled there is a tiny kernel of neural tissue. This nugget of nerves is smaller than a peanut and yet the pineal gland holds the key to your body's biological clock.

Although it is no Big Ben, the pineal gland is an accurate time-keeper. The mainspring of this clock is a storehouse of that all-important neurochemical, serotonin. In response to the day and night cycle of the earth, serotonin is converted to melatonin and then back again. This cycle of conversion takes twenty-four hours. The pineal gland coordinates the cycle to the day/night cycle of planet Earth. Noon on the outside matches noon on the inside of your body. The key to the accuracy of this biological clock is exposure to daylight. If it "sees" daylight regularly, the pineal gland will not lose time or gain time but will always cycle exactly in concert with the Earth as our planet whirls around in space.

You may take only a few seconds to set your wristwatch, but it takes three weeks to reset the pineal gland and your biological clock. This

123

biological clock adjusts your body chemistry for sleeping and waking. Every evening the pineal gland will set your body for sleeping, and you begin to feel drowsy. After you fall asleep, the pineal gland adjusts your body for waking, and you arise feeling refreshed.

But just what happens to your body while you are asleep? After falling asleep, you drift deeper and deeper into slumber, reaching a state of deep restorative sleep. Then you begin to drift into a lighter state of sleep and enter the dreaming state, or REM sleep. REM stands for "Rapid Eye Movement" because your eyes are actually moving around in response to your dreams as if you are following movement. After REM sleep, you start the cycle all over again on a ninety-minute rotation.

As the night progresses, the deeper sleep lessens, and the REM sleep increases proportionally. This cycling is of paramount importance in order for you to feel rested. Interrupt the cycle, and you interrupt the restorative power of sleep.

We have already learned that an alteration in serotonin function is seen in depression. It should be easy to imagine how low levels of serotonin can cause malfunction of this internal biological clock. Change the balance of serotonin, and you alter the biological clock. The result can be insomnia or excessive sleepiness. Both extremes can be seen in depression. And if you alter the sleep cycle, you change the entire energy level of your body. Without proper rest the body becomes sluggish.

Tools for Tomorrow

LifeFilter 20

Setting Positive "Stones" in My Life

"But one thing I do: Forgetting what is behind and straining toward what is ahead, I press on toward the goal to win the prize for which God has called me heavenward in Christ Jesus" (Phil. 3:13–14).

Today

1. I will make a list of attainable goals I can work toward that will help me conquer depression.

2. Remember: if I'm having sleep problems, read again and follow Dr. Hennigan's suggestions for sleeping better.

3. Confirm that the stones (goals) in my life are moving me forward in a positive way.

4. I will praise God for helping me move toward a wonderful future.

Problems with sleep associated with depression include:

- Difficulty falling asleep.
- Waking up in the middle of the night with difficulty falling back to sleep.
- Unusually brief periods of REM sleep.
- Unusually brief periods of deep, restorative sleep.

Another form of sleep dysfunction can be associated with depression. "Micro-awakenings" momentarily arouse you from sleep and never allow you to reach a deep, relaxed level of sleep. The next day your muscles feel sore and tight, and your joints ache.

What can be done to restore this delicate balance? Taking care of your depression will help restore the levels of serotonin in your body. As serotonin levels return to normal, your body's biological clock will reset itself. But you must be patient. Remember, it takes three weeks to reset the clock!

Also, a dietary supplement of melatonin has been reported to be helpful in restoring normal sleep patterns. It is not harmful to try melatonin, but you might want to consult your physician. Try to establish a normal sleep pattern whether you are too sleepy or an insomniac.

If all else fails, seek out a sleep clinic. These centers are established by neurologists who are experts in sleep disorders. Your sleep problems may be the result of something other than depression and, in fact, may be contributing to your depression.

Here are some other helpful hints:

- Don't exercise strenuously within two to three hours of retiring, as this can cause wakefulness.
- Don't eat a large meal within two hours of bedtime.
- Adopt a bedtime ritual such as an orderly progression of events leading up to bedtime. This ritual of brushing your teeth, locking the door, changing into your sleep clothes, and, perhaps, reading will create a comfortable progression into sleep.
- Avoid stimulants such as caffeine during the day.

If all else fails, see your physician for help in sleeping. Be aware that some sleep aids can actually alter the biological clock and cause more harm than good. But be patient. As your depression improves, so will your sleep life. And remember, your body rests best when you are asleep. Give your body the eight hours of rest it needs every night.

SUMMARY

Today we've added the weapon of setting goals to your increasingly powerful arsenal. This weapon not only gives you another way to defeat depression, but it also:

- Makes your tools work efficiently.
- Strengthens the medicines you take, making them more effective.
- Helps you fire your other weapons more accurately.

PHYSICIAN'S FACT

1. The pineal gland is the center of your body's biological clock.
2. Serotonin levels are important in keeping your biological clock on schedule.
3. Sleeping disorders may result from abnormal levels of serotonin.
4. Try to reach a balance between all of your body's normal functions, including sleep.
5. Consult your physician before considering sleep medication or dietary supplement with melatonin.

Setting goals helps you know you're making progress. It also shows the path your life is taking. Think of goals as stepping-stones: each one not only helps you get across a difficult stream, but it also shows where you've been.

It's important to know where the stones are in your life. For example, did you know you're putting down stones at this moment? Whether you realize it or not, the process of reading this book each day causes you to set—and reach—small goals. Look back through this book. Twenty firm stones form a path that leads you away from hopeless depression and toward a healthy emotional life.

That's twenty goals you've set and reached. Each goal is not only a stepping-stone, but it also becomes a part of the firepower in your arsenal, making you even more powerful and accurate.

DAY 21
Trusting God's Love

THE POWER TO WIN

Sue hummed to herself as she laid the dress out on the bed. A single parent, widowed for two years, it had been hard going to keep the bills paid and her ten-year-old daughter properly clothed. With a lot of work and a little luck, however, she had done it. Tonight was going to be a small reward for all the long hours. A bonus from her job had allowed her to buy the dress. An invitation to a party with some of her friends beckoned from the dresser. Sue hummed and smiled as she anticipated the evening.

"Mom, can I talk to you a minute?"

Sue turned to see her daughter briefly stick her head in the bedroom and then head to the kitchen. She followed. "What's up, Katie?"

"You know Sandra, don't you?" Katie asked. "She wants to know if the two of us can hang out at the mall for awhile tonight. That would be great, wouldn't it?"

Sue tried to be careful how she framed her answer. "Katie, you know I don't mind your spending time with Sandra. But I've already told you that going to the mall at your age without some supervision makes me uneasy. I trust you, but I don't trust some of the people you might encounter there." She picked up a memo pad. "Tell you what, give me Sandra's phone number, and I'll talk with her mother. Maybe one of us will be able to take the two of you to the mall later this week."

She was not prepared for Katie's reaction.

"I hate you!" the ten-year-old screamed. "You don't trust me, and you never let me have any fun. All the other mothers let their girls go to the mall. Why can't you?"

And with that Katie ran from the kitchen.

Sue shook her head and tried to calm down. She picked up her daughter's dirty dishes from the table, rinsed them off, and put them in the dishwasher. When Katie calmed down, Sue would talk to her daughter and try to discover why the girl had reacted so strongly. There had to be more beneath the surface than she was sharing.

Katie, running down the hall, was seething. Her mom didn't want her to have any fun! She cared only for herself! Didn't she see how she was hurting Katie?

Passing her mom's bedroom, she saw the dress lying on the bed. Here was a way to hurt her! Before she could really think about it, Katie picked up some scissors and began making huge cuts down the length of the dress. "There," she thought, "that should teach her a lesson!" Then she went to her own bedroom and waited for the punishment that would surely follow.

Fifteen minutes later, Katie realized her mother wasn't coming. She tiptoed down the hall until she could peek around the corner of the doorway. There was her mother, stretched out on the bed, face down, sobbing into the ruined new dress.

Instantly, Katie realized the horror of what she had done. Anger gave way to shame. Indignation fled in the face of embarrassment. Instead of the warm bond she usually felt with her mother, a cold wind seemed to push them ever further apart. Going over to her mother, Katie put her arms around her and said, "Mom, I'm so sorry. Take me back. Please take me back."

Have you ever blown it with God? Totally, radically blown it?

I have. And it made me feel cold and alone. Even after I'd asked God to forgive me, I still felt alone and unclean. After all, I reasoned, my sin was deliberate and enormous. I deserved to suffer. And, thinking like that, suffer is exactly what I did. The abundant life promised by Christ now seemed impossibly far away. My prayer life dwindled to nothing. Why should God listen to a miserable person like me?

Then I remembered the story of the prodigal son. Talk about someone blowing it! He took his inheritance (earned by his father, not him) and left against his father's will. He refused to take any responsibility for the farm, leaving more work for everyone else. And then he spent in a few weeks what it had taken his father a lifetime to accumulate.

From there, the prodigal son's life took an immediate plunge. Penniless and alone, he was reduced eventually to living, working, and eating in a pigpen—and the pigs were eating better than he was! Finally (his head must have been as hard as mine) he came to his senses. Cheeks blushing with shame, the wayward young man turned his steps toward home. Maybe his father would let him work and eat with the slaves. He knew it was all he could expect and more than he deserved.

As he turned the last curve that would bring him in sight of the house, a whirlwind hit him. The son found himself totally embraced by love. Let's let God's Word tell the rest of the story:

> "But while he was still a long way off, his father saw him and was filled with compassion for him; he ran to his son, threw his arms around him and kissed him.
>
> "The son said to him, 'Father, I have sinned against heaven and against you. I am no longer worthy to be called your son.'
>
> "But the father said to his servants, 'Quick! Bring the best robe and put it on him. Put a ring on his finger and sandals on his feet. Bring the fattened calf and kill it. Let's have a feast and celebrate. For this son of mine was dead and is alive again; he was lost and is found.'" (Luke 15:20–24)

The son, if you didn't realize it, is me . . . and you.

He didn't deserve forgiveness, but his father gave it to him. That's called *grace*.

He was absolutely bowled over by the love of a father who was watching every minute for his son to return. That's the *love of God*.

And upon his return, he was given more than he could have ever expected. That's called *restoration*.

Earlier in this book I told you that one of the most valuable lessons I've learned is to trust in God's Word, not my emotions, as my final authority. When the two don't agree, it's my emotions that need changing, not the Bible. And when I finally quit letting emotions dictate my spiritual temperature, I became able to accept God's undeserved forgiveness. The abundant life he promised gradually became a part of my daily experience.

God took me back.

Are you like me? Have you done something that haunts you in those quiet moments when you're alone? If so, the story of the prodigal son—which is the story of God's forgiveness and love—is for you. All he wants is for you to return and acknowledge your wrong.

If you decide to do this, be sure to look up quickly. You'll discover a heavenly Father rushing to embrace you in his love and forgiveness. In fact, he's waiting for you right now.

And don't worry. He *will* take you back.

STRENGTH FOR TODAY
Dramatic Change

I sing solos. I act in dramas. I speak easily in front of hundreds with no fear or nervousness. In my heart I am a natural-born ham.

Why then was I cringing in fear in my bedroom with the door locked, listening to the voices in the den? Why did my heart race with terror whenever the phone rang? Why did I peek out the front windows of my foyer before racing across the den to the kitchen in fear someone would be at my front door? Why would I wander aimlessly around a shopping mall for hours avoiding going home for fear someone outside my family would be waiting for me?

I was depressed. It was the worst episode I had ever experienced in my forty years of life on this planet. All it took was one well-deserved remark and my entire world—no, my entire universe—crumbled around me. All the carefully constructed excuses and works and obligations and dreams fell apart like so much wet paper.

There is no need for me to go into the details. Suffice it to say my life collapsed, and nothing was left. I awoke the next morning with a heavy, loathsome beast crouched on my chest. His name was Fear. I avoided personal contact with any of my friends, including my pastor, Mark

Sutton. In a letter I resigned from all my obligations at church. I refused to talk to anyone. I withdrew into a comfortable, safe, dark cocoon of depression.

How could such a dramatic change come over me, Mr. Outgoing Personality, Mr. Take-the-Center-Stage, Mr. Confident Leader? Depression is that powerful. It is the David that slays the Goliath, the mouse that frightens the elephant, the spark that ignites a consuming fire.

I tell you this because I have been there. If you are depressed, I _know_ how you feel. I've had the unreasonable fear, the sleeplessness, the loss of energy, the sheer feeling of wanting to do absolutely nothing but just fade into my surroundings. Let me repeat. I know how you feel!

> Why do bad things happen to good people? Because bad things happen to God's people. It is his way of growing us, refining us as iron sharpens iron.

Why do bad things happen to good people? Because bad things happen to God's people. It is his way of growing us, refining us as iron sharpens iron. It is God's way of putting us through the crucible of suffering so we can be there for someone else who is in need, someone else who may not have the access to the Savior we have. At the time this doesn't make the suffering any easier. And, when you're in the midst of it all, you can't see God's big picture. You're merely trying to survive. In today's devotion I want to share one tool with you that helped me defeat depression and remains a tool for keeping the beast at bay.

The foundation of the doctor/patient relationship is the H&P. Those letters stand for _history_ and _physical_. The first thing a doctor does when he meets a patient is to communicate with him/her and obtain the history of the patient's illness. The doctor asks questions that allow him to cover systematically all of the possible symptoms of any disease. Then the doctor performs a review of systems, asking questions pertinent to each organ of the body. Finally, the doctor touches the patient, prodding, poking, listening as he completes the physical examination.

Early in my counseling I obtained a journal. On one side of the page was a short devotion for each day of the year (in my case excerpts from

My Utmost for His Highest by Oswald Chambers), and in the adjoining column space to write my thoughts and feelings. I would end each day by reading my Bible verse and the devotion. It was amazing how God had set up each selection to speak to me about the events I had been going through on that day! In the empty space I would jot down my thoughts about my day, analyzing my wayward thought patterns. Then, like the sun dawning on a new day, I would discover new insights in light of God's Word. Some days I would be so down I could only read and merely scrawl, "God help me." Other days the victory would be so sweet I would run out of room to write. The key was discipline, following a plan every day to do something about my depression.

Like the H&P, there were three parts to my daily entries. Reading the Bible verses was like taking a history. By looking at the world through the eyes of the Bible, God's words from the past, I could ponder my own immediate past. What mistakes had I made this day? What sins were in my life? Where had I taken my eyes off Jesus?

The review of systems would become reading the devotion, an orderly progression through a system of interpreted Scripture. The devotion always took me from the beginning to the end, from the general to the specific, from confusion to truth.

And, finally, the physical examination of my own personal soul took place as I poured out my heart onto the written page.

As the weeks progressed, I would be able to look back on events in my past. When I was undergoing a particularly stressful day, I could review my past and see that I had actually made significant changes in

---

Tools for Tomorrow

LifeFilter 21

My Guide to Restoration after Failure

"So he got up and went to his father. But while he was still a long way off, his father saw him and was filled with compassion for him; he ran to his son, threw his arms around him and kissed him" (Luke 15:20).

Today

1. I will remember that God loves me even when I fail.
2. I will believe that my heavenly Father is always waiting, with open arms, to take me back.
3. I will repent of what I've done and ask God's forgiveness.
4. I will begin a daily spiritual H&P. I will write in a journal containing a daily devotion. It's good preventive medicine.

---

my life. It also reminded me that God helped me through those difficult times. I was a survivor! All this made my current problems seem smaller and more manageable. After a year, I retired the journal and started a new one. I discovered depression came to visit less and less often. And, when it did, it stayed for shorter periods of time. Whenever the unwelcome visitor arrived, I could take up my journal and revisit the suffering of my past and the victories God gave me over depression. I took my own spiritual H&P! Such an analysis always managed to put my current problems in the proper perspective.

Today depression still lingers at the edge of my life. But it is an infrequent intrusion. And when it does hit, it bounces off quickly. Routinely, however, I dust off the old H&P of my past illness and recall a time when I was sick. Rereading my journal is good preventive medicine. I am learning from my past and avoiding repeating my mistakes.

Want a good suggestion for defeating depression? Take a daily spiritual H&P and write it down in a journal that contains a daily devotion. It's good preventive medicine.

SUMMARY

Why do bad things happen to good people? Because bad things happen to God's people. It is his way of growing you, refining you as iron sharpens iron. It is God's way of putting you through the crucible of suffering so you can be there for someone else who is in need, someone else who may not have the access to the Savior you have.

But what happens if you fail to see God in your suffering? What are the consequences of taking your eyes off God and giving in to your depression? Will God forgive you? Can you return to his arms?

If you're asking questions similar to these, the story of the prodigal son—which is the story of God's forgiveness and love—is for you. All he wants is for you to return and acknowledge your wrong.

If you decide to do this, be sure to look up quickly. You'll discover a heavenly Father rushing to embrace you in his love and forgiveness. In fact, he's waiting for you right now.

And don't worry. He *will* take you back.

Part 5

The Exit Signs That Lead You Out of Depression

Susan and I lived and worked in France for a number of years. During that time we grew to love both the people and the culture of that beautiful country. But that didn't stop it from also being the scene of one of the most terrifying events I've ever experienced. It happened about two weeks after our arrival.

We lived in the suburbs of Paris during our first year in France. Driving in that huge city was, to say the least, an interesting experience. Lanes were merely "guidelines" that could be ignored with impunity. Couple that with the fact that when I first moved to France I spoke not a word of the language, and you have a recipe for disaster.

One day, I somehow discovered that the first American-style football game ever to be played in France would take place at 8:30 the next night on the other side of Paris. It would mean about an hour's drive through unfamiliar streets, but I decided my navigational talents were up to the task. That turned out to be one of the dumbest decisions I've ever made.

We were living in Massy, a small town just south of Paris. When I left the next night, a Michelin map lay on the seat beside me, and precise directions on how to get to the stadium were firmly fixed in my head. Sure enough I drove right to my destination, found my seat, and had a great time watching the French try to figure out American football. About midnight the game concluded, and I returned to my car. The "journey of terror" was about to begin.

I opened the map, plotted my return course, and pulled out of the parking lot. It seemed that everyone else in the stadium parking lot was going in the same direction as I was. Surrounded by what I was sure were thousands of cars, I headed for the six-lane road that was the "loop" around Paris. Once there, I knew the trip would go smoothly.

Wrong again.

At about the halfway point on the way home, I suddenly encountered a "Detour" sign. This was something I hadn't counted on, but I had no choice but to get off the route I knew and follow the other cars. After a few kilometers, however, I came to a traffic circle with about six roads offering choices. Cars branched off in all directions. *They* knew the way home; I did not. To top it all off, there were no more detour signs to guide me! The Michelin map on the seat seemed to think I was in unknown territory—none of the road signs I saw were in this edition.

By this time I was deep in the French countryside at 1:30 in the morning. Nothing was open. The streets were deserted. I knew no one else in all of France. And, to top it all off, our family did not yet have a telephone. Even if I had been able to find someone to talk to, I couldn't have communicated what I wanted or understood their response.

I was completely, totally lost.

Have you ever had a wave of panic reach up and consume every part of you? That's what happened to me that night. I absolutely did not know what to do or where to go. *Calm down!* I told myself. *You've got to calm down and think positive.* I looked at the gas gauge: it was almost full. That was positive. Then I looked toward heaven: God was there, and he knew how to get me home, even if I didn't. Lifting a very sincere prayer to the Lord, I chose a road at random that looked like it headed back toward Paris and began what I hoped was my return to familiar territory.

Everything was dark and lifeless on that road. I saw no other cars, no streetlights, not even any policemen. Thoughts of spending the night in the car began flitting through my head. If I didn't come home, my wife would think something bad had happened. She didn't speak the language, either. Plus, she had a preschooler and no telephone—a horrible combination! Panic began trying to take control again, and I knew if something didn't happen fast I was going to lose what little peace I'd managed to gain.

Without warning a big blue sign loomed up out of the darkness. "MASSY: 10 Kilometers," was emblazoned on it. I think it must have been the most beautiful message I had read throughout my entire life! Just like that, everything changed. A familiar exit sign led me immediately from despair to hope. Following its directions, I soon found my way home to safety and light and warmth.

Have you ever been lost? Do you ever feel as if your life is without direction? Do you want to begin moving toward happiness and light? Over these last nine days together, Dr. Hennigan and I will be giving you more strong encouragement as your teammates. But we will also be providing you with a map that can lead you out of depression and unhappiness. As you read, please follow the directions carefully toward freedom and a new outlook on life.

DAY 22
Leaving Solitude and Finding a Counselor

The Power to Win

At a critical point in the game, I noticed our players were tired. They were also beginning to make mistakes. If they continued playing the same way, the team would lose. I signaled for a time-out and called the players to the bench. Quickly I told them to sit down and rest while I diagrammed a different defense and some new plays. When the whistle blew to restart the game, the team was rested and had a plan to win. From there on, the game was ours.

I love sports. ESPN and I are old friends. So you might be wondering what kind of athletic team I coach.

I don't.

In the first paragraph I wasn't talking about baseball, basketball, football, or any other type of team sport. Instead, I was talking about the biggest game of all: *life!* The players could have been a husband and wife at a difficult time in their marriage. Or they could have been a couple struggling with the debilitating effects of depression and unhappiness.

Are you someone who thinks talking to a counselor is unneeded? If so, think of a counselor as a "coach." Think that's farfetched? In any game the players are so involved on the field or court that they are often unable to see how the flow of play is developing. They may have begun "grooving in" some bad habits that will hinder them. Or they may simply be tired. A good coach watches carefully from the sidelines and understands the players' problems. When he or she spots a weakness, the coach quickly calls a time-out and allows the team some time to rest while getting them back on the right track.

A good counselor does the same thing. He or she can see, from the sidelines, the flow of your life. Unbiased, they can give you both time to rest and good advice on how to get your life back on track. Because they have seen a lot of "teams" and watched a lot of "games," their experience can guide you and help you avoid the same mistakes others have made. In short, a good counselor can help you win the game of life.

There's another good reason for using a counselor: the Bible recommends it! Let's take a look at several Scriptures, beginning with a description of Jesus Christ: "For to us a child is born, / to us a son is given, / and the government will be on his shoulders. / And he will be called Wonderful Counselor, Mighty God, / Everlasting Father, Prince of Peace" (Isa. 9:6).

Yes, Jesus Christ, himself, is the greatest Counselor of all! His wisdom and insight into life are revealed to us in the Bible. The more we read it, meditate on it, and absorb it, the better we will be able to handle all that life throws at us.

But God says he has given us others to help us, as well.

One of our allies is the local church. Our heavenly Father has decreed that we find other brothers and sisters in Christ and develop meaningful relationships with them. Together we help one another, and together we worship God.

Part of developing meaningful relationships with other Christians is being willing to share problems and doubts with them. Again, as I've said once before, be careful with whom you share. Make sure they are positive, mature Christians who can take what you say, continue to love you, and give you the benefit of their wisdom. But do share. The Christians I've just described are out there, and God has given them some wonderful abilities to help people just like you.

"Bear one another's burdens, and so fulfill the law of Christ" (Gal. 6:2 NKJV).

In other words, as you share your problems, doubts, and burdens, you not only allow other wise Christians to use the gifts God has given them, but you also *allow them to fulfill the law of Christ!* And remember: they can't bear if you don't share.

Finally, God gives some people a unique ability to "read" people and help them with their lives. Jesus Christ, Wonderful Counselor, has also given earthly counselors to help us through the difficult passages of life. Look at what God's Word has to say about them and your own life: "Where there is no counsel, the people fall; / But in the multitude of counselors there is safety" (Prov. 11:14 NKJV). "Without counsel, plans go awry, / But in the multitude of counselors they are established" (Prov. 15:22 NKJV).

> Part of developing meaningful relationships with other Christians is being willing to share problems and doubts with them. And remember: they can't bear if you don't share.

According to God, trying to make it through this world alone is to be doomed to failure. Without counselors, people can fall morally and spiritually. Without wise counsel, your plans in life can fail. God has given you his Son, Jesus Christ, as the ultimate Counselor. He has given you the local church, with some wise Christians in it, to help you in your daily walk. And he has gifted some people as counselors to help you with especially difficult times.

Don't turn away from any gift of help God offers you! If you need help with your depression or unhappiness, let someone gifted in the area of counseling use his or her gift to help you move back into the light. Make today the day you leave your solitude behind.

Strength for Today
Behave Yourself

I sat in my car, watching the car windows frost over from the cool November air. Across the street the house sat nestled among trees whose fiery red leaves were giving way to the inevitability of autumn. The house had two stories and a huge front porch built in the days when sitting outside and visiting with neighbors was a vital part of everyday life. I watched a porch swing move gently in the fall breeze and saw movement through the large windows. If I didn't know better, I could imagine a family going about their normal evening routine, sitting in front of the fireplace, talking about the events of the day, anticipating the promise of the future. I knew this was not the case. Within this house dwelled endless pain.

With growing terror and trepidation, I stepped out of my car, drew a deep breath, and took the first step in a journey that would change my life forever. Inside the warm living room a smiling woman greeted me from behind a sliding glass window.

"I'm Doctor . . . ," I paused, feeling vulnerable and conspicuous. I glanced around at the young couple sitting nervously on the couch. On the love seat an older woman dabbed at her nose with a tissue, her eyes staring off into the unknowable distance. This place was the great equalizer. Here titles and degrees and social stature meant nothing. Here we were all struggling for answers to our individual problems. I gave my name to the woman and sat stiffly in the corner, ready to bolt out of the room at any minute. I didn't need to be here. I didn't need this kind of help. All I needed was some time, and I could handle these problems on my own. There wasn't anything wrong with me. I wasn't crazy!

My thoughts were interrupted by a smiling man, his bright blue eyes alive with energy, his smile genuine. He motioned me up the stairs, and I climbed out of my old world into a new one.

Later I will share more of my decision process in seeking professional counseling. Suffice it to say, it took years of concerted pleading on my wife's part to make me finally go. In the two years that followed, I never regretted making that first climb up the stairs.

Is professional counseling an option for you? Should you talk to someone? Absolutely. Without a question. No doubt about it.

Who, then, should you talk to?

Freud started it all. Since then the field of psychological therapy has mushroomed, and you may be puzzled by all the choices. I want to help you understand the array of possibilities available to you and the professionals involved in the process of counseling.

A psychiatrist is a doctor with a medical degree who can write prescriptions, overseeing the medical aspects of mental health. After graduating from medical school, a psychiatrist will go through a residency program in psychiatry, three to four years in length. For those illnesses requiring hospitalization, the psychiatrist heads up a team of workers who join together to help the patient through his or her illness.

A psychologist has a master's degree or bachelor of science degree in psychology. Sometimes a psychologist will pursue a Ph.D. in psychology and will be referred to as a doctor. Psychologists are trained in methods of behavioral therapy or psychotherapy. They do not write prescriptions and do not oversee the medical problems of their patients.

Social workers also have a similar degree to psychologists and help the patient adjust to social conditions. Professional counselors, such as pastors, have special training in counseling and exposure to the principles of behavioral therapy.

Where do you start?

- If you are a member of a church, start with your pastor. A pastor may feel qualified to counsel you in your depression or may recommend a consultation with someone with more expertise.

> ### Tools for Tomorrow
>
> #### LifeFilter 22
>
> *I Can Dilute My Depression through Sharing*
> "Where there is no counsel, the people fall; but in the multitude of counselors there is safety" (Prov. 11:14 NKJV).
>
> #### Today
> 1. Remember: God does not want me to be alone in this world. That's why he is always with me.
> 2. I resolve to leave isolation and share meaningfully with some positive, wise Christians.
> 3. If necessary, I will find a godly counselor and let him/her partner with me in overcoming my depression.

- You may choose a counseling center. Counseling centers use professional counselors or psychologists.
- If you have seen your physician, he may advise a course of therapy and refer you to a counselor or psychologist.

What then can you expect from your counseling session?

Two types of therapy exist. The age-old psychotherapy is based on techniques developed by Sigmund Freud. Psychotherapy traditionally deals with repressed childhood experiences with which the patient must deal in order to achieve relief. Today psychotherapy has been trimmed down to "talk therapy."

143

The most commonly used technique is cognitive therapy. Cognitive refers to thought processes. Cognitive therapy is a powerful self-help technique for dealing with depression and other negative emotions by *consciously changing the way we think.*

What are the benefits of seeking professional counseling? First, the counselor, in most cases, does not know you. You can share anything on your mind without fear of being judged. Second, the counselor is trained in techniques to determine when you are not being truthful with yourself. The counselor holds up a mirror to your behavior in order to help you become aware of your own behavior patterns. Third, the counselor is there to help you. He or she is not there to ridicule you or condemn you. You are paying the counselor to help you. That is his or her job. For the hour you are sitting in that office, the counselor's whole reason for existence is to help you and you alone. No distractions. No hidden agendas. No fear of rejection. Fourth, the counselor is unbiased in the ability to appraise your behavior. He or she can ask telling questions that make you think about your behavior in a totally new light. Gaining a different perspective on your pattern of thinking and behavior is the basis for overcoming depression.

After two years of counseling, I walked away from that antebellum home a different person. And the counseling stuck. I internalized the changes. Before I went to counseling, depression was a constant companion, striking without warning and crippling me for days as I struggled to overcome it. During the two years of counseling, I learned to recognize the trigger events in my life that brought on bouts of depression. I saw the train coming before it hit me. Now, after four years, I've learned to stay off the tracks. Depression still haunts me, but it's infrequent. And when it comes, I have a step-by-step method for dealing with depression and overcoming it.

Depression no longer controls my life. And you can keep it from controlling your life as well.

Make a decision today to talk to a counselor if you haven't already. Don't waste years of needless misery because you are too proud to admit you need help. It will be the best walk up the stairs you've ever had.

SUMMARY

According to God, trying to make it through this world alone is to be doomed to failure. Without counselors people can fall morally and spiritually. Without wise counsel, your plans in life can fail. God has given you his Son, Jesus Christ, as the ultimate Counselor. He has given you the local church, with some wise Christians in it, to help you in your daily walk. And he has gifted some people as counselors to help you with especially difficult times.

Don't turn away from any gift of help God offers you! If you need help with your depression or unhappiness, let someone gifted in the area of counseling use his or her gift to help you move back into the light. Make today the day you leave your solitude behind.

PHYSICIAN'S FACT

1. Various Christian professionals are available to help you with professional counseling.

2. By analyzing your behavior patterns, you can make life-changing alterations in your way of thinking.

3. Gaining a different perspective on your pattern of thinking is the basis for overcoming depression.

DAY 23
Leaving the Indoors and Discovering God's World

The Power to Win

The two couples going out to eat had been married for years. As they got into the car, the men sat in the front, the women in the back.

"Jim, where are we eating tonight?" Frank asked from the passenger's seat.

"We're going to our favorite restaurant," Jim replied. "It's called . . . ," he hesitated a long moment, then shook his head. "Help me out here. What's the name of the flower that's red and has thorns?"

"A rose?" Frank ventured.

Nodding his head, Jim said, "That's it!" Then, briefly turning his head toward the backseat, he looked at his wife and said, "Rose, what's the name of that restaurant?"

It's so easy to forget!

Earlier this week I was visiting with a senior adult couple. The husband is one of the finest artists I've ever seen, and I was admiring his paintings and awards. Eventually the conversation turned to physical problems, and the wife told me her husband was seeing a wonderful doctor.

"What's his name?" I asked.

She paused a moment. "His name is . . . ." Then she laughed and said, "You'll have to excuse me; I'm having a 'senior moment.'"

Forgetfulness is a common problem for most of us in at least one area of our lives. Some people can't remember names; others have trouble remembering numbers; details escape regularly from the memories of many great thinkers; and "I'm sorry, dear, I forgot what you sent me to the store for" has been a part of many couples' conversations.

So think of today as a reminder of something you already know but may have forgotten. Remembering this bit of information, and then acting on it, can sometimes take away your depression immediately, lift your spirits, and make you feel better all day long.

> Depression wants to keep us inside and alone. It thrives on the dark.

What is this miracle fact? It's called "the outdoors." God created it for your enjoyment and amazement. But when is the last time you availed yourself of God's gift to you?

Depression wants to keep us inside and alone. It thrives on the dark. Solitude and four walls are its allies. If it can relegate you to the bedroom, depression will grow stronger.

Sunlight, on the other hand, treats depression the same way it treats Dracula in books and movies. Once exposed to the bright light of day, both the mythical monsters and the real disease vanish into nothingness.

It's time for you to leave the indoors and discover God's world. Your depression will try to stop you. It will help you think of all kinds of excuses to keep from weakening it. But remember, you've already learned that together you and God are stronger than your depression. So say no to your emotions and get out into the sunlight.

How often should you try to get outside? As often as possible. At least once every day that the weather permits, you should move outdoors and participate in God's great creation. Think of your emotions as a plant. The more sunlight you receive, the better your spirits will grow and the more beautiful your life will bloom.

Once you find yourself outside, what should you do?

I have a confession. I'd like you to think I'm 6 feet 2 inches, about 185 pounds, in whipcord shape with almost no extra body fat. In reality I'm shorter than 6 feet, and if I ever reach 185 pounds, my family will think I've become anorexic. The moment I was born, the doctor took one look at me and said, "Put that baby on formula and SlimFast!" Since that moment, I've been on some kind of diet nearly all my life. A snail could outrace my metabolism. If I don't eat right *all the time,* I gain weight immediately.

You get the picture. But why am I telling you this?

I'm giving you this information because after knowing my body type, what I'm about to tell you should create an even greater impact on you: Exercise is one of God's ways of treating your depression.

Now believe me: I'm not one of those guys who loves to live at the gym and pump iron. In fact, I have to grit my teeth to make myself work out. And even after I'm done, I still resemble the Pillsbury Dough Boy more than I do Arnold Schwarzenegger. But I've come to realize that my body gets a real lift from regular, sweat-producing exercise. I might be tired when I begin working out, but by the time I'm finished—and especially about an hour later—I can feel more energy coming into me. As I go through the day, my emotions are higher, my attention better, and my ability to make decisions stronger.

In short, exercise works!

I'm not saying you have to lift weights or spend hours doing aerobic exercises. But anything—long walks, jogging, basketball, swimming, or any other sport—can help raise your heart rate, your energy level, and your mood.

Your body is important; don't neglect it. The Bible says: "Do you not know that your body is a temple of the Holy Spirit, who is in you, whom you have received from God? You are not your own; you were bought at a price. Therefore honor God with your body" (1 Cor. 6:19–20).

"Honor God with your body." Certainly this means living a morally pure life. But you can also use those words as the impetus to begin a regular program of exercise. In doing so, you give Jesus Christ, and yourself, a better temple in which to live.

Let me leave you with two rules that act as a reminder of what you've learned today:

Outdoor Rule 1. Give each day to God. As the sun shines down on you, you'll find God's Son also shining down on you. The sun dissipates the shadows of night. The Son destroys the shadows of depression.

Outdoor Rule 2. The higher you raise your heart rate in exercise, the higher you raise your spirits.

STRENGTH FOR TODAY
Move It!

The mountains soared above me, arching their green, rocky spines toward a perfect blue sky. I moved with the grace of an Olympic runner, my legs slicing through the cool air, my lungs filling with life-giving oxygen. A perfect moment in time and space, my mind at peace from a "runner's high." San Diego stretched away beneath me as I ran along a road on the mountain ridge. In the far distance the ocean sparkled with foam. I could not imagine being anywhere more wonderful.

I never saw the rock.

Perhaps a small boy had thrown it at a snake along the path; or perhaps a tremor in the bedrock of the earth had dislodged it from the perch where it had resided for

> At the University of California at Berkeley, School of Public Health, an ongoing survey clearly shows a strong association between a sedentary lifestyle and depression.

millennia, awaiting my arrival. The forces of nature conspired against me to place the rock perfectly under my foot.

I fell across the running path, pain lancing up my left leg. Nausea clouded my vision, and the pain was unbearable. As my eyes cleared and the perfect clarity of the moment faded with the growing pain, I glared at the rock, a tiny stone that had felled me. Later, I learned I had stepped on the rock and twisted my ankle so severely I would have to maneuver around San Diego in a wheelchair. My running days were temporarily at an end.

At this time in my life, I had been jogging three miles a day for almost a year. In the weeks after the injury, as I returned from my vacation, other people noticed a change in my personality. I became agitated and angry from the least provocations. I seldom smiled and would reply to inquiries with the demeanor of a mad pit bull. I was not totally unaware of the changes in me. I noticed I had trouble sleeping, difficulty concentrating. In short, by giving up on my daily exercise, I had become angry, agitated, and depressed. It was as if I were withdrawing from a powerful drug.

In fact I was. The "drug" was exercise.

The most dreaded word in the English language must be the *E* word. I am not speaking of exorcism, although most people would rather be exorcized than exercised!

Why do we dread the idea of exercise? Most likely it is because we have become a sedentary nation, plopped down on our couches in front of the cable television or glued to the Internet. At the University of California at Berkeley, School of Public Health, an ongoing survey clearly showed a strong association between a sedentary lifestyle and depression. However, studies have shown that exercise is necessary, in fact almost mandatory, in the battle to defeat depression.

> One study showed that twelve weeks of jogging was as effective in relieving depression as twelve weeks of psychotherapy.

Why did I become depressed when I could no longer exercise? Why is exercise so essential to overcoming depression? You may recall an earlier discussion of the "economy of movement" that comes with depression. Remember how the body slows down as the synaptic pathways from the brain fail to function properly? Scientists have discovered a substance called *endorphin*. Endorphin has an effect on the brain similar to the effect achieved when a person takes a narcotic such as morphine. In fact, narcotics work on the endorphin-stimulated areas of the brain.

Endorphin is released by the nerves working with the exercising muscle to limit the pain associated with exertion. Studies have shown that the exercise of muscles also increases the levels of serotonin in the brain and can have an effect that may last for two weeks! The combined effects of elevated serotonin and the euphoric effects of endorphin give you a relaxed, stress-free feeling. One study showed that twelve weeks of jogging was as effective in relieving depression as twelve weeks of psychotherapy. If exercise is so important, how can you avoid the negative stigma associated with the *E* word?

The main concept is movement. Movement and physical activity will produce the same changes in your brain chemistry. At a minimal level, twenty to thirty minutes of sustained activity such as walking, jogging, or swimming three to four times a week will bring about the desired results. Other studies have shown that cumulative small episodes of physical activity can have the same benefit.

If you are loathe to exercise, then try walking up and down the stairs instead of using the elevator. Park at the far end of the parking lot and walk a longer distance to your work or to the store. Look for every available opportunity to move. You will be surprised how the time can add up and bring about the desired improvement. Of course, always consult your physician before starting any exercise program.

A word to the wise: be patient. Studies have shown it takes at least a month of sustained exercise to notice a significant mood-elevating effect. Also, remember this isn't competition. Your exercise program should be enjoyable. Take it nice and easy, and don't increase the strenuousness or duration of your workout more than 10 percent a month. Exercise shouldn't be a chore. It should be fun!

Tools for Tomorrow

LIFEFILTER 23

Honoring God with My Body
"Do you not know that your body is a temple of the Holy Spirit, who is in you, whom you have received from God? You are not your own; you were bought at a price. Therefore honor God with your body" (1 Cor. 6:19–20).

TODAY

1. Weather permitting, I will get outside and enjoy the sunshine God made for me.
2. I resolve to begin (or continue) a regular program of exercise.
3. I will stop and thank God for sending his Son, Jesus Christ, to forgive my sins and live with me forever.

An interesting study regarding the motivation for exercise points out a significant difference in the way we approach our movement. Contrary to popular belief, this study demonstrated that people who exercise regularly year in and year out are not motivated by the desire to control weight or improve their physical appearance. They do not respond to negative goals. Rather, they have a desire to seek the reward of consistently feeling relaxed, focused, and alert. These people stick with their exercise because exercise brings on a sense of pleasure and contentment. This study showed that regular moving released tension, counteracted depressed feelings, and combated food cravings. Make the decision to take up some form of movement, and you will feel better after the first effort.

You don't have the time? Wrong!

We never *have* the time to exercise. The point of this study is that desire is the important ingredient. If you are motivated to exercise out of a sense of obligation, then you will never *have* the time. Something else will always be more important. But if you desire to exercise, then you will *make* time.

No time? Make time!

PHYSICIAN'S FACT

1. Exercising is a proactive response to your depression; deciding to move will have a lasting benefit on your mood.

2. Exercise is a pleasant distraction from depression; it gets you out into the world and away from your sheltering darkness.

3. Exercise has positive effects on your physical and mental health.

4. Exercise has a sustained, positive effect on your serotonin and endorphin levels, elevating your mood and helping you overcome depression.

5. No time? Make time!

SUMMARY

Depression wants to keep us inside and alone. It thrives on the dark. Solitude and four walls are its allies. If it can relegate you to the bedroom, depression will grow stronger.

Sunlight, on the other hand, treats depression the same way it treats Dracula in books and movies. Once exposed to the bright light of day, both the mythical monsters and the real disease vanish into nothingness.

"Honor God with your body." Certainly this means living a morally pure life. But you can also use those words as the impetus to begin a regular program of exercise. In doing so, you give Jesus Christ, and yourself, a better temple in which to live.

DAY 24
Leaving Old Habits and Making New Ones

The Power to Win

What habits do you need to break?

Before you begin making a list, consider this. Chances are, there are some strong habits of which you are completely unaware. And they might be the very ones holding you back from a healthy emotional lifestyle! So let's take an inventory. Get out a piece of paper, grab your pencil, and get ready to think and write.

Wait just a minute. I know what you may be thinking: *This is hard. I'll do it another time; maybe tomorrow.* You can't put this off until another time and continue to get better. Don't make excuses; make a list! Here are some thoughts to get you started.

- Am I maintaining any relationships that push me toward negative thinking and depression?

Does God want you to give up these relationships? Are there people you know who cause you to begin thinking in the wrong way? Or, if it's a relative, can you put a little space between you and him/her from time to time? (I'm not talking about a spouse, here. If you're having marital problems, get my first book, *Thirty Days to a Better Marriage*).

- Do I engage in some activities that tend to make me depressed? Can I give them up?

My friends still laugh at me about the way I gave up golf. I'm a pretty hyper person, and about eight years ago I was surprised to find myself making excuses about why I couldn't go play eighteen holes with my friends. After analyzing my reaction, I finally saw that the four hours I spent playing golf was a huge block of time I didn't want to give up. Also, the game didn't move fast enough to keep me from thinking about things at the office. The result was that I came home from the course tenser than when I started!

One beautiful spring day I was playing on a championship course with three good friends. I had just hit a four iron to the edge of the seventh green, and my partner revved up the cart to move us in that direction.

"Larry, pick up my ball, please," I said.

Larry was startled. "Why? What's going on?"

"I'm quitting golf," I replied.

"When?" Larry was becoming more and more puzzled by my behavior.

I grinned and said, "Right now. And I don't think I'll play it ever again until I retire." With that I got out of the cart, walked to the car, and drove away with a lighter heart than I'd had in a long time. With one exception (for a church tournament) I've not played in the last eight years.

Do I think golf is wrong? Of course not! In fact, I still watch it on television and follow it in the sports pages. But golf was wrong for me and my mental health.

It may be an innocent activity, but if something you're doing causes you to be stressed or depressed and you can quit it, then do so.

- Have I paid attention to the things that enter my mind through my eyes and ears?

Television. Are the television programs you watch helping you toward a healthy mental outlook? If you watch the daytime soaps, for example, understand that the subject matter is overwhelmingly negative. Secure marriages are seldom presented. Truth and positive lifestyles are in short supply. A steady diet of programs like this can soon make you believe they represent a normal life. The trash talk shows are even worse. Hype, not help, is the subject of these programs. I'm convinced every day you spend watching one of these shows moves you closer to depression. Can you change your daily viewing schedule? Or even better, can you eliminate it altogether and replace the viewing time with something more positive and less passive on your part?

Movies. Are you indiscriminate in what you watch when it comes to movies? Whether at the theater or at home on cable, a host of movies are available that cover dark subject matter and present a terrible morality. Watching these shows cannot make you a happier person or a better Christian. Can you be more selective in what you watch?

Books. What I read stays with me a long time. I can remember scenes from favorite books I read twenty years ago. Books are powerful. If you read the wrong type, however, you allow an insidious enemy entry into your mind. Once there, it can affect you long after the book is finished and the pages have been closed. On the other hand, good, encouraging books can also stay with you a long time, working throughout your mind, heart, and emotions to make you a stronger person. Can you choose better books to read and put down the trash?

Music. Do you ever find yourself humming a tune without realizing it? Music is also a powerful medium. Because the tune can be catchy or beautifully melodic, the message attached to it may stick firmly in your mind. Is the music you listen to moving you closer to God or further away from him? Should you change your listening habits?

• Identify time wasters.

Admittedly, we're beginning to get into the subtle areas of your life now. Time wasters, however, cannot only slow you down; they can also contribute to your stress level and depression. When you realize you're not going to be on time or you no longer have the time to do an important task, guilt and disgust are waiting in the wings of your mind to take control of your emotions.

One of these time wasters controlled my life for a long time and I didn't even know it. I was getting ready for work one morning when Susan came through the bedroom and said, "Mark, you're depressed today, aren't you?"

She was right. But the depression hadn't started until I'd gotten up that morning, and we'd been in different parts of the house until that moment. How did she know?

Susan quickly enlightened me. "You've been sitting on the side of the bed for twenty minutes with socks in your hand. You always do that when you're depressed. It takes you forever to put on your shoes and socks."

What? I was shocked and, if the truth be known, indignant. "Honey, I don't do that all the time when I'm depressed," I protested.

"Of course you do." Susan is compassionate, but she is also truthful. "You dress quickly until you get to this point. Then you simply sit and stare—sometimes for what seems like forever—if I don't push you a little."

Believe me, from then on I began trying to monitor my behavior closely when depressed. And sure enough, Susan was right! (By the way, she's usually right.) If I wasn't careful, my whole life crawled to a halt while I engaged in navel gazing for long periods of time.

We've already learned that identifying a problem helps rob it of its power. That's exactly what happened in this case. Because I'm now aware of this potential time waster, putting on my shoes and socks is actually the *fastest* part of my getting ready in the mornings!

I once knew a CPA who was a brilliant, hard worker. She had built up a large firm and was considered successful. So I was surprised to see her enter my office one day and begin pouring out a sad story. Haltingly, she admitted to severe depression. Her practice was suffering because she could get nothing done. The woman would find herself sitting at her desk with hours having passed without her knowledge. Unfortunately, that was early in my ministry, and I'd not yet begun to learn about how to treat and conquer depression. If I could see her today, one of the things I'd try, after counseling and medicine, would be to ask her about the time wasters in her life. We would identify them and begin tracking them. Once exposed to the light, I'm convinced time wasters can be conquered.

The above questions and suggestions should be enough to get you started making a good list of habits (both conscious and unconscious) that, taken away from your daily life, will actually enrich you. Start writing!

How did you do? Are there other habits you need to add to the bottom of your list?

The exercise you're currently completing is significant. That's because identifying the problems is at least half the battle. You can't fight an enemy you don't know or can't see. Once it's put down on paper, however, you begin robbing the bad habit of its power.

In Psalm 119:37, we have these words of wisdom: "Turn my eyes away from worthless things; / preserve my life according to your word."

Let your eyes—and your ears, mouth, feet, and hands—turn away from worthless, time-wasting, guilt-inducing habits.

As you begin cleansing your life of these distractions, you are better able to see one of the exit signs blinking in your life, offering another way to leave the power of depression behind forever.

Take a moment to ask God's help with any habits that need to be eliminated from your life. You might want to pray:

> Dear God, here are the bad habits I've identified. If there are any others I need to be aware of, please show them to me now. As best I can, I give these habits to you. Please take them away from me and replace them with good, healthy habits. Thank you for hearing this prayer and starting me on the right path. And thank you for loving me in spite of my weaknesses. In Jesus' name, Amen.

STRENGTH FOR TODAY
Find Balance

Ulysses had to resist the call of the sirens, their voices urging him into their hungry arms. My sirens were imprisoned safely out of sight, but I knew exactly where they were. They called to me, their promise of fulfillment so powerful an image in my mind that I abandoned all logical thinking. I drifted from the bedroom to the kitchen. I was getting nearer! I could almost feel them in my hands, taste them on my lips. The brownies cried out for their freedom from bondage!

My wife had made them, and for days I had avoided them. After a week the brownies were dry and stale, and my wife threw them into the trash compactor. Their broken bodies were trapped beneath the flattened lettuce and discarded potato peels, reposing at the bottom of the trash. I pulled out the trash compactor and reasoned only a day's worth of trash lay between me and the brownies. Yes, I dug them out of the trash! And yes, I ate them! Voila! I washed them down with milk!

I sat in the darkness of my room after that and wondered what on earth had possessed me to dig old, dry brownies out of the compactor. I seemed to be a man on the verge of starvation. My actions made no logical sense. For my entire life submission to this temptation was an ongoing sin. In my attempts to avoid overeating, I had been on every diet known to man, and then some. I had tried it all, and food was the only thing that soothed me. In my moments of deepest, dark despair, food would always be my friend. It filled my emptiness.

After a lifetime of battling the bulge, I have learned what science has only begun to discover about the craving for food. It all goes back to our old friend, serotonin. When we are under stress, depressed, tired, or dieting, our bodies crave certain foods needed to restore the levels of serotonin.

Since serotonin must be replenished every day and is not a stored substance, our bodies need the building blocks. We have already learned that depression occurs with low serotonin levels, so it should be no surprise that alterations in our appetite also occur.

In depression weight gain is common. This is not necessarily because of increased consumption of food. Remember how serotonin controls the balance of our bodies? With low levels of serotonin, our metabolism slows down, and we store more food as fat. Since we are also moving less and burning up fewer calories, weight gain occurs.

Sometimes weight gain occurs even though the appetite is depressed. How can this be explained?

Serotonin restores balance in the brain chemistry. Certain nerves, however, act as inhibitory neurons. When stimulated, these nerve cells actually produce chemicals to slow down the transmission of nerve impulses. They are the brakes that keep the delicate balance of stimulation and inhibition intact. Imagine driving through heavy downtown traffic. To avoid ramming the car in front of you and to avoid the blaring horn of the car behind you, you maintain a constant back-and-forth pressure between braking and accelerating to keep you moving at precisely the right speed. Your brain functions the same way. When the serotonin levels are out of balance, more inhibitory neurons may fire, therefore depressing your appetite centers. The result is a decreased appetite instead of an increased appetite. In depression it is possible to have both conditions.

How then can you restore this delicate balance and have a more balanced appetite? Here are some ways in which you can take steps to control your appetite.

Foods to avoid:

Sugar. I hate to say it, but sugar is your worst enemy. Sugar is absorbed quickly by the body and drives your insulin levels up. Insulin is secreted by your pancreas to control the level of sugar in your blood. The problem comes when your sugar plummets in response to insulin and you become low on blood sugar. You feel shaky, hungry, depressed, and your only hope is to, you guessed it, eat more sugar. On and on you go on this endless cycle of sugar high and sugar low. Insulin promotes storage of sugar as fat and makes matters worse. The real problem is how it makes you feel. Sugar lows can mimic the feelings of panicky depression. Avoid sugar or use it sparingly. I strongly recommend the *SugarBusters* diet as an alternative.

Caffeine. Caffeine quickly goes to the brain and stimulates the nerve cells. It is a quick pickup. But caffeine can be mildly addictive, and once it is gone can cause a downer. Also, caffeine interferes with sleep and your biological clock. Indirectly it affects your serotonin levels. Use it carefully.

Tools for Tomorrow

LIFEFILTER 24

Making the Best Use of My Time

"Turn my eyes away from worthless things; preserve my life according to your word" (Ps. 119:37).

TODAY

I will . . .

1. Look carefully at my habits and give up any that are not God honoring.
2. Identify and remove time wasters that keep me from having a good outlook on life.
3. Feel better by eating better (and healthier).

Alcohol. Although alcohol may actually boost serotonin levels, it ultimately is dangerous because it depresses brain function overall. If you are depressed, the last thing you need is more brain depression!

How can you beat these food-binging blues? Here are some suggestions:

1. When you get a craving, wait four to twelve minutes to see if the hunger passes. If it does, then the craving is a psychological one and not biological.

2. Recognize your trigger foods—those foods that prompt a chain of eating and binging. Avoid them when you get the munchies, and eat something else instead.

3. If you want to eat because you are bored, distract yourself by calling a friend, taking a bath, or going for a walk.

4. Eat five small meals a day instead of three big ones. This keeps your intake on a more balanced level and may actually help to restore those serotonin levels.

5. Keep your blood sugar steady. Eat more complex carbohydrates such as cereals, rice, pasta, bread, and potatoes. Or, better yet, go on *SugarBusters*. Avoid the ups and downs in your blood sugar.

6. Eat more vegetables. Eating more vegetables definitely can increase your levels of serotonin by supplying more of the chemicals needed in serotonin production.

7. Take a good multivitamin and mineral supplement. It doesn't matter which kind. Just take any one of the vitamin supplements you can find at your grocery store.

8. Finally, exercise. The dreaded *E* word! Exercise can reduce your food cravings and keep you on a more even metabolic keel.

Depression is bad enough, but to have difficulty with weight gain and the attendant low self-esteem can be devastating. Don't try to lose weight while you are depressed. Focus on your psychological well-being and try to maintain your weight. When you get out of the depression, then you can concentrate on weight loss. Once you begin losing the weight you have gained, your self-esteem will skyrocket, and you can feel good about yourself. Only then can you successfully resist the call of the hidden brownies!

Summary

In Psalm 119:37 we have these words of wisdom: "Turn my eyes away from worthless things; preserve my life according to your word." Let your eyes—and your ears, mouth, feet, and hands—turn away from worthless, time-wasting, guilt-inducing habits.

As you begin cleansing your life of these distractions, you are better able to see one of the exit signs blinking in your life, offering another way to leave the power of depression behind forever.

Take a moment to ask God's help with any habits that need to be eliminated from your life. You might want to pray:

> **PHYSICIAN'S FACT**
>
> 1. Serotonin levels can determine your appetite.
> 2. Depression can cause either increased or decreased appetite.
> 3. Be aware of food triggers and avoid them.
> 4. Don't worry about looking good and losing weight while you are depressed.

Dear God, here are the bad habits I've identified. If there are any others I need to be aware of, please show them to me now. As best I can, I give these habits to you. Please take them away from me and replace them with good, healthy habits. Thank you for hearing this prayer and starting me on the right path. And thank you for loving me in spite of my weaknesses. In Jesus' name, Amen.

DAY 25
Leaving Your Failures and Discovering Your Blessings

THE POWER TO WIN

Matthew Henry's *Commentary* has blessed and informed thousands of Christians for decades. Many years ago, Henry was held up and robbed. That evening he made the following entry in his diary: "Let me be thankful—first, because I was never robbed before; second, because although they took my wallet, they did not take my life; third, because although they took my all, it was not much; and fourth, because it was I who was robbed, not I who robbed."[1]

Is it any wonder Matthew Henry became a spiritual giant who influenced generations of Christians? Early in life he learned to look for God's exit sign that showed the way out of the rooms of guilt and anger.

If he had wanted, Henry could have engaged in endless speculation after the robbery. *If only I'd been more careful, this wouldn't have happened. God must be punishing me for some sin I'm not aware of. I never should have had this much money on me. I'm just not supposed to feel safe in this world.* And the list goes on and on until guilt has swept in and covered the whole incident with paranoia and self-recriminations.

Others, whom we'll call perpetual victims, might have said this about the incident: "Doesn't that robber know I needed that money? I'll hate him until the day I die. I'll relive this incident over and over, and I'll tell my friends about it until they're sick of the subject. After all, my friends should have been with me this evening. I was alone, so it's their fault for not being there. Come to think of it, God could have stopped this, but he didn't. It's really all his fault. I'm so angry."

Guilt and anger. For many people these are the only emotions they generate in response to their own failures and trials. Isn't it interesting that in reading the Book of Acts, little of either emotion is found:

1. Stephen, a godly man, is stoned to death. As he faces the end of his life, all he reveals is compassion for his accusers and joy at being able to suffer for Christ.

2. Peter and John are put in prison for talking about Jesus. They are threatened with death, beaten, and finally released. Did they go straight to their lawyers to sue? Of course not! Instead, they went straight to the temple to praise God for allowing them to suffer for him.

3. James the Apostle is killed. Barnabas is beaten. Paul is stoned, shipwrecked, and imprisoned. None of these men even begin to question themselves or God concerning the pain they've suffered. Instead, all look forward to a future with God. The past, with its mistakes, is given to Christ. The present is lived with full attention to the marvelous, everyday possibilities of God's wonders living in his children.

Let me ask you a question: How do you treat your own failures, mess-ups, and mistakes? Do you agonize endlessly over them? Do you chastise yourself repeatedly and build layer upon layer of guilt in your life?

Now for another question: How do you react to things that are done to you unfairly? Do you become angry and unwilling to forgive? Do you engage in long pity parties for days or weeks at a time? Does your family have to tiptoe around you when you're in one of your moods?

Depression thrives on guilt and anger. They are the meat and potatoes of this debilitating condition. But don't despair! I'm getting ready to show you several exit signs that lead directly out of the gloomy, joyless rooms of guilt and anger.

Guilt's exit sign is found in Isaiah 43:25: "I, even I, am he who blots out / your transgressions, for my own sake, / and remembers your sins no more."

In other words, when you bring your sins to Jesus Christ and ask for forgiveness, he does just that. But in addition he also blots them out and remembers them *no more!* Isn't that great! No more guilt or recriminations about how you did wrong at some point in your life. No more tears over lost opportunities. No more losing the "what if" game over and over.

If God forgets your sins, don't you think it's about time you did too? Let go of the guilt and embrace a future with God in control and ready to bless you.

Now, what about the anger? Here's what God has to say about this insidious, joy-sapping emotion: "And when you stand praying, if you hold anything against anyone, forgive him, so that your Father in heaven may forgive you your sins" (Mark 11:25).

Do you realize how radical a command Jesus makes here? Everything anyone has ever done to you must be forgiven. You can't hold grudges in your heart or bricks in your hand to use against others. A clenched jaw or a clenched fist is not compatible with being in God's will. But the bottom line is this: *As long as you don't forgive others, you won't receive God's forgiveness!*

Think about that for a moment. You can go to church, contribute heavily, teach a Bible class, even preach glorious sermons from a pulpit. But if you harbor an unforgiving spirit, none of those other deeds means anything! You must forgive others to be forgiven!

Decide right now to begin forgiving everyone. That doesn't mean you allow people to walk all over you; nor does it mean you condone what's been done to you. It does mean that you will no longer keep the memory of what these people have done to you close to your chest. Instead, you both free yourself from the chain of hatred, and you turn the people who have hurt you over to God's care. Believe me, he can deal with them far better than you can.

Guilt and anger. Some stay locked in these rooms all their lives, never seeing God's exit signs glowing in the emotional darkness.

You have been shown where the exit signs are. Now what are you going to do with that knowledge?

Dear Lord . . .
Please grant that I shall
Never waste my pain; for . . .
To fail without learning,
To fall without getting up,
To sin without overcoming,
To be hurt without forgiving,
To be discontent without improving,
To be crushed without becoming more caring,
To suffer without growing more sensitive,
Makes of suffering a senseless, futile exercise,
A tragic loss,
And of pain,
The greatest waste of all. — Dick Innes[2]

STRENGTH FOR TODAY
Get Over Being Sad

I dread the winter months. In my profession of radiology, I have learned there is an inherent fear of radiation by most hospital planners. The safest place, in their minds, is in the basement surrounded by feet of dense concrete. Therefore, I find myself confined to the dark and gloomy windowless environment of the basement, victim of a superstitious fear. I usually come to work early in the morning while it is still dark. And in the winter months I do not leave until after sunset. In fact, I can go an entire workweek without seeing the sun!

I have noticed during those weeks that I develop a mild, unrelenting depression. For years I did not realize this form of depression was purely biochemical. It is known as Seasonal Affective Disorder or SAD.

SAD: Seasonal Affective Disorder

SAD has been linked to shorter days and the decreasing amount of sunlight to which a person is exposed. SAD generally begins in late autumn and continues into early spring.

People with SAD experience:

- Extreme fatigue and lack of energy.
- Inability to focus or concentrate.

165

- Increased need for sleep.
- Carbohydrate craving and weight gain.
- Feelings of depression.

Studies have linked SAD and shortening days with changes in serotonin levels in the brain related to the pineal gland (see day 20).

SAD can be treated by exposing yourself to more light. Using bright lights in the workplace is effective. Going outside two to three times a day during the workday and taking a short walk can help. If SAD is severe, it may require medication. Remember, the cause is purely biochemical, not behavioral.[3]

Tools for Tomorrow

LifeFilter 25

Forgiveness: Accepting It and Giving It

"I, even I, am he who blots out your transgressions, for my own sake, and remembers your sins no more" (Isa. 43:25).

Today

1. Believe: that when I ask God, in Jesus Christ, to forgive my sins, he will do it!
2. Let go of guilt and anger.
3. Forgive anyone who has wronged me. I will ask God to help me forgive.
4. Go outside: let God's sun and God's Son warm my life.

Dysthymia

"There has never been a day of my life when I didn't feel depressed," a friend of mine once told me. In fact, he has lived his entire life troubled with chronic, unrelenting depression. His depression, astonishingly, is not debilitating. And at times he suffers from a major depressive episode on top of his chronic depression. He suffers from dysthymia.

Dysthymia is a chronic, low-grade depressive state. If this state persists for longer than two years, the diagnosis can be made of dysthymia. The danger is that most of these people function, albeit with a lot of extra effort, fairly well in life and may not recognize their condition. Quite often the gloominess and irritability are perceived as a part of the person's personality. The good news is, dysthymia responds every bit as well to counseling and medication as severe depression. The challenge is in recognizing it.[4]

Depression in Women

Women place more emphasis on interpersonal connection and relationships than men. Although this can be a powerful and positive characteristic, it can also make some women more vulnerable to depression when these relationships fail to develop. In fact, one-fourth of all women are likely to experience depression. It is important, therefore, for women to learn to recognize the signs of depression and seek medical help. This is particularly true of depression related to changes in hormonal function. Not only do women experience monthly changes in hormone levels, but they also experience the devastating effects of menopause. Hormonal treatment or replacement may help alleviate depression related to these causes.

Depression after childbearing is a special problem for women. Studies have linked the "post baby blues" to the plummeting levels of estrogen and progesterone hormones. For some women, feelings of depression may linger even after hormones have returned to a normal level. Medication and/or counseling may be necessary to overcome this type of depression.

SUMMARY

Decide right now to begin forgiving everyone. That doesn't mean you allow people to walk all over you; nor does it mean you condone what's been done to you. It does mean that you will no longer keep the memory of what these people have done to you close to your chest. Instead, you both free yourself from the chain of hatred, and you turn the people who have hurt you over to God's care. Believe me, he can deal with them far better than you can.

PHYSICIAN'S FACT

1. SAD: Seasonal Affective Disorder is caused by shorter days and little exposure to sunlight.
2. Dysthymia can be a chronic, unrelenting, low-grade depression, but it is treatable.
3. Women suffer greatly from various forms of depression and respond well to therapy.

Guilt and anger. Some stay locked in these rooms all their lives, never seeing God's exit signs glowing in the emotional darkness.

You have been shown where the exit signs are. Now what are you going to do with that knowledge?

Part 6

Three Attitude-Affirmers That Stop Depression from Starting

Walter Wangerin Jr. is one of my favorite writers. He has a way of telling stories in beautiful prose that gently point to great truths. In his book *Mourning into Dancing*, Wangerin tells of a time when, as a boy of eight, he thought his dad was the strongest man in the world. "He was a handsome man in those days. He had a curl of hair at the middle of his forehead, and brown eyes, and a pulsing muscle in his jaw. And he loved me. So I would go out on the front porch and roar to the neighborhood: 'My daddy's arm is as strong as trucks! The strongest man in the world.'"

Wangerin goes on to tell how he loved to climb into a great cherry tree in their backyard and read for hours. Sometimes he became so engrossed in a book that he failed to notice when the weather changed. . . .

. . . One day suddenly, a wind tore through the backyard and struck my cherry tree with such force that it ripped the book from my hands and nearly threw me from the limb. I locked my arms around the forking branches and hung on. My head hung down between them. I tried to wind my legs around the limb, but the whole tree was wallowing in the wind.

"Daddy!"

The sky grew absolutely black. Dust whirled higher than the house. I saw a lightning bolt drop from heaven, then there was a perfect calm, and then the thunder crashed.

"Daddy! Daddy! Daddy!"

The whole tree bowed down and rose again, and the wind blew my shirt up to my shoulders, and the rain hit like bullets, and I thought that my arms were going to slip from the branches.

"Daddeeeeeeee!"

There he was. I saw his face at the back door, peering out.

Lightning stuttered in the sky.

"Out here! Up here! I'm here! Daddy, come get me!"

The branches swept up and down, like huge waves on an ocean—and Daddy saw me, and right away he came out into the wind and the weather, and I felt so relieved because I just took it for granted that he would climb right up the tree to get me.

But that wasn't his plan at all.

He came to a spot right below me and lifted his arms and shouted, "Jump."

"What?"

"Jump. I'll catch you."

Jump? I had a crazy man for a father. He was standing six or seven miles beneath me, holding up two skinny arms and telling me to jump. If I jumped, he'd miss. I'd hit the ground and die.

I screamed, "No!" At least I could feel the bark of the branches against my body. "No!"

I made up my mind. I'd stay right here till the storm was over. I closed my eyes and hung on.

But the wind and the rain slapped that cherry tree, bent it back, and cracked my limb at the trunk. I dropped a foot. My eyes flew open. Then the wood whined and splintered and sank, and so did I, in bloody terror.

No, I did not jump. I let go. I surrendered.

I fell.

In a fast, eternal moment I despaired and plummeted. This, I thought, is what it's like to die—

But my father caught me.

And my father squeezed me to himself. I wrapped my arms and legs around him and felt the scratch of his whiskers on my face and began to tremble and began to cry. He caught me. Oh, my daddy—he had strong arms indeed. Very strong arms.

But it wasn't until I actually experienced the strength that I also believed in it.

And I myself did not choose so frightening an experience. The storm did.

Horrible storm. Wonderful storm.

It granted me what I had had all along, but what I had not trusted. A father with arms as strong as trucks.[1]

Five days to go.

We have five more days together. I want us to use this time to the max. If you haven't already done so, Bruce and I are going to try our best to transform how you feel about depression. We want you to experience God's love for you. And we want you to experience it every day.

In Wangerin's story of the storm, it was not until he experienced the fury of the winds and the terror in his heart that he could finally, truly, experience the strength and love of his father.

I want you to come to the same conclusion about your depression. For it has been in depression's deepest moments in my life that I have discovered the depth of God's love for me. Instead of standing outside my depression beckoning to me, he has descended into the maelstrom to be with me; to whisper encouragement to me; and, ultimately, to lead me safely into the light once again.

171

It is in this depression not of my choosing that I have discovered the strength of my heavenly Father. And in doing so, I can truly say I've been blessed.

How have I learned to do this? One of my greatest helps has been what I call "attitude affirmers." Over the next three days I'll share them with you, as well. They could keep some of you from even having depression! For the rest of us, it will be a way to minimize and control what used to control us.

DAY 26
Every Day: Believe God Loves You

THE POWER TO WIN

Does God love you? Right now, in this place, can you feel his love?

One of the greatest problems depressed people face is a difficulty believing God loves them. Interestingly, they have no problem believing God loves *other* people. But somehow, they believe the promises of the Bible are not for them.

Am I describing you?

If so, it is vital that you discover, believe, and put into use this particular attitude-affirmer.

Let's begin with a basic understanding: *the reason you may believe God doesn't love you has nothing to do with God and everything to do with your depression.* The Bible has literally hundreds of passages where God declares his love for you. It's not necessary to be perfect to receive God's love and to be in his will. All it takes is repentance and a desire to be close to him.

Here are several personal messages from God to you. Let's begin with: "For I am convinced that neither death nor life, neither angels nor demons, neither the present nor the future, nor any powers, neither height nor depth, nor anything else in all creation, will be able to separate us from the love of God that is in Christ Jesus our Lord" (Rom. 8:38–39). That ought to cover just about any excuse you can come up with about why God might not love you!

If you're still doubtful, listen to Christ as he speaks of God's love for you: "The Father himself loves you because you have loved me and have believed that I came from God" (John 16:27).

Need more convincing? Worried you might not live up to God's love? Do you feel your life doesn't measure up to deserving these promises?

> The reason you may believe God doesn't love you has *nothing* to do with God and *everything* to do with your depression.

Then read this last love letter from your heavenly Father (who, by the way, never lies and always keeps his word!): "But when the kindness and love of God our Savior appeared, he saved us, not because of righteous things we had done, but because of his mercy" (Titus 3:4–5a). "Not because of righteous things we had done, but because of his mercy." Did you see those words? That means he loves you!

Dan Livingston was desperate. Terribly overweight, he had tried every diet that came along. Alas, the weight was still there and getting worse. He finally made an appointment with his physician and asked for help.

The doctor had a unique idea for Dan. "I want you to eat normally for two days, then skip a day. Repeat this schedule for two weeks and then come back to see me. By that time you should have lost five or six pounds."

Two weeks later Dan returned to the doctor's office. His physician was shocked to discover his patient had lost more than forty pounds!

"How in the world did you do this?" he asked.

"Doc, I just followed your instructions. But to tell you the truth, I thought I was going to die before I finished the two weeks."

"Were you that hungry?"

"No!" Dan replied. "But that skipping all day nearly killed me!"

Any day in which you skip believing God loves you is a day in which you invite depression and guilt to take over. So come back to the above Scriptures every day if necessary. Carry the LifeFilter at the end of this chapter with you every day for awhile as your constant reminder of God's love. No attitude-affirmer is stronger than remembering that, at every moment, you are surrounded by the awesome love of God.

Do I practice what I preach? You bet I do. When I turn my digital phone on every morning, I have programmed it to begin with this message: "Today God loves you!" The screen savers on my desktop computer and on my laptop proclaim God's love for me. And I regularly listen to music that speaks of God's love.

What can you do to remind yourself of this important attitude-affirmer? The more you discover and believe in God's unfailing love for *you*, the more difficulty depression will have pulling you into its clammy grip.

Believe it: God loves *you!*

STRENGTH FOR TODAY
StressBusters

Welcome! Do come in and have a seat. I'm sure you're in a hurry to rid your life of unwanted stress, so I'll get right to the point. I am Dr. A. Drenalin, and I am the founding president of StressBusters. When you are stressed out and feeling tired and frustrated, who are you going to call? StressBusters! Well, I am sure you've seen our commercials. Forgive my enthusiasm, but I do want to help you.

In order for us to be of assistance, we have to get an idea of the level of stress you are experiencing. We here at StressBusters have developed a simple and painless survey to determine your level of stress. Just take a look at this list and answer a simple yes or no. Then we'll tally up your score and see just how stressed you are.

- Do you feel like you have to throw cold water on your face at dinner or breakfast to wake up your mind because you're wiped out from getting less than six hours sleep?
- Do you have an older parent who needs your care; or do you have one or more children either under the age of six or over the age of thirteen?
- Do you wake up feeling someone has added more chores to your to-do list while you were asleep so that your tasks are never done?
- Do you regularly use the horn in traffic, even when the guy in front instantly heads through the green light? Do you regularly

lose your temper as a response to the guy in the car in front of you?

- Do you wish you were in Congress so you could ban all national holidays, birthdays, anniversaries, grandparent's day, secretary's day, and all those other "needless" (in your mind) celebrations that add more work for you?
- Do you multitask, that is, operate in more than two roles daily or often find yourself doing several things at once?
- Do you find yourself forgetting important things like keys, money, appointments, directions, or even your own name and address, because you're always in a race against the clock?
- When you're tired and need a boost, do you reach for that hidden stash of yummies tucked away in an inconspicuous hiding place only you are aware of?
- Are you in an unhappy relationship at work or at home?

We have a simple scale to rate your score. If you scored less than two yes answers, then you have the secret to a happy, balanced life, and you need to join our staff! If you answered yes to three to five of the questions, then you are dangerously close to being overbalanced and under considerable stress. If you scored six to seven, you are significantly stressed and running on fumes. If you scored greater than seven, then you are running out of fuel and are close to empty!

How did you do? Are you stressed out? If you are, that isn't surprising. A 1995 survey showed that 30 percent of workers feel stressed every day; 40 percent feel daily moderate stress; and 43 percent had visible physical or emotional problems from stress. Just existing day to day in modern America is stressful.

What? You say you are depressed? It's no wonder. Stress is one of the leading causes of depression. Would you like to know why?

Inside your brain is a chemical called serotonin. Oh, you've heard of serotonin? Good, then you understand its role in keeping your brain in balance. When life is smooth and not stressful, your serotonin levels can keep up with the mild everyday activities. But when too much stress is placed on the brain, serotonin production can't keep up with the demand. Important nerve centers slow down and malfunction. The whole brain becomes distressed, and the person enters a state of brain-chemical imbalance. The person feels overwhelmed by life and may complain of fatigue, inability to sleep, aches, pains, lack of energy, and depression.

Now do you see how the stress in your life is contributing to your depression?

Not to worry. Here at StressBusters we have a perfect prescription for dealing with stress: PEACE. That's P.E.A.C.E. Before I give you a prescription, I need to make an appointment for you to see Dr. Burnout promptly tomorrow morning. From your score you need his ministrations as badly as you need my prescription.

Now let's get on with the cure!

People. Develop good people skills. Learning how to relate to people better can reduce stress. Also, rely on people as confidants and friends. Remember, no man is an island. We need one another. Surround yourself with people you can trust and rely on. And then talk to them. One of the best ways to learn people skills and talk about your depression is to join a support group.

Education. Learn all you can about depression. Learn how your body and brain coexist in the healthy state as well as in the stressed-out state. Read books and articles. Consult your physician and search the Internet. The more you know, the quicker you can conquer depression. As Albert Einstein once said, "Never stop questioning."

Action. Be proactive. Don't wait for someone to come along and remove your depression. Take action. Go to your doctor. Get off the couch and move. Involve yourself in outside activities. Be active and you will find that depression will be easier to defeat.

Tools for Tomorrow

LIFEFILTER 26

Believe in God's Love

"For I am convinced that neither death nor life, neither angels nor demons, neither the present nor the future, nor any powers, neither height nor depth, nor anything else in all creation, will be able to separate us from the love of God that is in Christ Jesus our Lord" (Rom. 8:38–39).

TODAY

1. Remember that God loves *me!*

2. Take a moment to thank God for his love and for his salvation.

3. Use PEACE (day 26) to find peace while overcoming depression.

Creativity. Be creative. Find a hobby. Hobbies stimulate your mind and cause you to think in different ways. By occupying your mind with these stimulating activities, you alter your brain chemistry. Learn to draw or paint. Take a gardening class. Learn a foreign language. Go to the museum. Stimulate your mind and "color outside the lines." Dare to be different.

Exercise. Daily movement is essential to defeating depression. You must get off the couch and move. Develop a daily routine of some kind of movement, even if it is walking up the stairs instead of using the elevator. Exercise of some kind is essential in defeating depression.

Well, there you have it. A prescription for dealing with your stress and overcoming depression. Try a little bit of PEACE every day, and you will find true peace from your depression, thanks to StressBusters.

SUMMARY

Any day in which you skip believing God loves you is a day in which you invite depression and guilt to take over. So come back to the Scriptures in this chapter every day if necessary. Carry the LifeFilter at the end of this chapter with you every day as your constant reminder of God's love. No attitude-affirmer is stronger than remembering that, at every moment, you are surrounded by the awesome love of God.

PHYSICIAN'S FACT

1. Stress is a part of every-day living.
2. Stress can deplete levels of serotonin and cause depression.
3. Develop a strategy to find PEACE from stress and depression.

DAY 27
Every Day: Focus on the Needs of Others

THE POWER TO WIN

Mark Twain once said, "The good Lord didn't create anything without a purpose, but the fly comes close."[1]

What is your purpose in life? God has certainly put you here for a reason. Over the next several days we will be exploring how you can lead a full, meaningful life using the talents and gifts God has given you. So let's begin with helping you break out of your shell of depression.

Joseph Scriven was happily and deeply in love with a young woman. He proposed marriage; she accepted. As plans matured for their wedding, Joseph's joy seemed to grow daily. Then just days before the wedding, tragedy struck. His fiancée drowned.

Scriven fell into bitterness and a deep depression for months. At his worst point, however, he turned to Christ and found grace and peace. Shortly afterward, this young man used his own gifts to touch the others in this world who, like him, had suffered tragic losses. He penned a hymn that is still blessing people around the world: "What a friend we have in Jesus, all our sins and griefs to bear!"[2]

How did Scriven leave his depression behind? Through a combination of looking to Christ *for* help and looking for others *to* help. And there are always others who can use your help. No matter how little money you have, there are others who have even less. No matter how depressed you are, there are others doing even worse. No matter how few friends you may have, there is someone who is achingly alone.

Your attitude-affirmer for today suggests that you go in search of these people. Discover their needs. Then use your own gifts and resources to help put their lives back on track. In the process of doing this, you will find your depression fading in strength. It will be replaced by a feeling of satisfaction and completeness. Why? Because in helping others you are doing what God has placed you here on Earth to do.

Could you get in the habit of doing this every day? I'm not suggesting that you'll always find someone to help. But simply by training yourself to look outside your own neediness toward the needs of others, you can begin holding depression at bay.

Charles Simpson illustrates this principle for us: "I met a young man not long ago who dives for exotic fish for aquariums. He said one of the most popular aquarium fish is the shark. He explained that if you catch a small shark and confine it, it will stay a size proportionate to the aquarium. Sharks can be six inches long yet fully matured. But if you turn them loose in the ocean, they grow to their normal length of eight feet."

Depression encourages us to keep to ourselves. It wants us to focus only on our own needs. Believe me, depression's siren call is seductive. There within its dark, quiet environment, it is easy to engage in endless speculation of your own life and its myriad problems. If you succumb too long to depression's seductive emotions, however, you'll find yourself smaller emotionally, less developed as one of God's children, content to live out your life in the frigid, dark waters of a small pond.

Could the above paragraph be talking about you? If so, it's time to break out of the pond and discover the wonderful depths of the ocean of life. Use the attitude-affirmer "Every day, focus on the needs of others" to grow in God's love. In doing so, you'll discover you're not the only one in this world who needs love, patience, and a kind word. And when you give each of those to someone in need, your heart and spirit will grow deeper, higher, wider, and happier.

STRENGTH FOR TODAY
Tired of Being Tired

Good morning and welcome to today's clinical session. Most of you know me, Dr. Burnout, and today we have a patient referred by StressBusters who seems to have an alarmingly high level of stress resulting in depression. This patient is concerned about lack of energy and unrelenting fatigue. I have asked for a written account of the most recent stressful episode, and we will now review the report.

"My heart began to pound so hard I thought it would burst from my chest. It made no sense for me to feel this way; my day had ended, and I was in the bed headed for slumber land. Pain lanced beneath my sternum. I was having difficulty breathing. At the age of forty, I was having a heart attack! After all, I am a doctor, and I should know.

"My wife sat up in bed next to me and smiled as she placed a reassuring hand on my chest. 'You're just exhausted. You're not having a heart attack. Can't you remember having a normal EKG treadmill test just last month?'

"I hate it when my wife uses logic! Nevertheless, the pain increased, and I saw my life slipping away before me.

"Just that morning I had headed a major regional drama conference at my church. That evening, I had been the producer and writer for a major drama presentation that involved almost one hundred people at my church. On the previous two days I had taken calls for my radiology practice and had received less than four hours sleep in two nights. In the past week I had worked ten hours each day and had come straight to the church each night until midnight to get ready for the drama presentation. On top of all that, I had been a father to my children, a teacher to my Sunday school class, a vice chairman to a church committee, and had gotten my mother out of the hospital after treatment for a major illness!

"It seemed my wife was right. I was exhausted! All that had taken place in one week. No wonder I felt like I was about to die. In fact, in just a few weeks after this night, I would burn out and descend into the worst depression of my life. The warning signs were all around me, and I did not see them."

Sounds like a typical case of burnout. For our client's benefit, let us review the definition of my namesake.

I would define *burnout* as simply cramming forty-eight-hours-worth of work and activities into twenty-four hours. In the process you become exhausted, overextended, overworked, and overwrought. You wake up the next morning miserable and unhappy and vow that today will be different. But by the afternoon, today is just like yesterday. Before you know it, this unending cycle will lead you to depression.

> I would define *burnout* as simply cramming forty-eight-hours-worth of work and activities into twenty-four hours. In the process you become exhausted, overextended, overworked, and overwrought.

How does this work?

As I have discussed several times, lack of energy can lead to depression. In today's society of Internet, cable television, cellular phones, fax machines, twenty-four-hour drive-throughs and power lunches, we burn our candle at both ends. We burn up the mental and physical energy set aside for a day's worth of normal living in a matter of hours.

All that serotonin gets gobbled up. All those nerve synapses get tired and depleted. And the only restorative is the thing most of us regard as a necessary evil: sleep.

Recent studies show that more than half of Americans who work for a living are either borderline burnouts or already burned out. Our society is destroying us by literally burning up our energy reserves until all that is left is depression.

Here is my advice on how to avoid burnout and retrieve all of that lost "energy":

- *Take control of your time.* Select just one area of your disorganized life and write out a cleanup schedule. Focus your life down to the few absolutely necessary tasks and begin to cross out those items on your schedule you can live without. You'll be surprised how many items on your to-do list are urgently calling for your attention but are really not important.

- *Learn to say no.* Christians believe there are many good ideas to pursue. Service is a hallmark of the Christian, but many often say yes to all those good things they can do. However, just because an idea is a "good" thing doesn't mean it is a "God" thing. Learn to discern between those things you could do for God and those things God wants you to do for him. Focus your spiritual life on the "God" things.

- *Delegate, delegate, delegate.* Instead of doing so much for your children, whom you feel you've neglected, get them to help out around the house. Don't confuse quantity time with quality time. Thirty minutes of focused attention is worth an hour of hurriedly cleaning up their room and harping on their failures.

- *Sleep, sleep, sleep.* We need at least eight hours of sleep a night yet we get less than six. Plus, sleeplessness is cumulative. In other words, if you lose an hour of sleep a night for a week, by the weekend you're five hours behind, and the only way to make up for it is to sleep an extra five hours. To understand how important this is, understand that sleep is the only way to restore those precious neurochemicals you've depleted. Even the best antidepressant can't undo loss of sleep. So plan wisely to sleep wisely. If you must, take a nap in the middle of the day. Plan it, and the short break will make you a much better person.

Tools for Tomorrow
LifeFilter 27
Looking Beyond My Own Needs
"Carry each other's burdens, and in this way you will fulfill the law of Christ" (Gal. 6:2).
Today
I will . . .
1. Thank God for meeting my needs.
2. Look for an opportunity to help other people.
3. Identify the activities and thought patterns causing stress in my life and try to change them.

- *When you find yourself harried and barking at those around you, take a time-out.* Walk outside and look at the sky. Sit down in the corner, and read a magazine for five minutes. Break the chain of frustration by doing something totally opposite to the frantic pace around you. At my hospital I have learned to go to the chapel five minutes every day and simply sit and let my mind be at rest. It is surprising how much peace God can give you in five minutes!

- *As someone has said, "Get rid of that stinking thinking!"* Be aware of your negative thoughts such as guilt, shame, and anger. Work on isolating those thoughts and counteracting them with positive thoughts. If you give in to the problems, you become a problem-oriented personality. Instead, become a solution-oriented personality. Look at problems as opportunities for improvement. This is a "paradigm" shift, a substantial change in the way you look at a situation. In other words, the glass is half full!

- *Finally, move!* Don't just walk fast or talk fast. Get out and walk around the block. Take the stairs and count how many steps you make to the next floor. In other words, take little doses of exercise throughout the day. Look for opportunities to divert that frantic, nervous feeling into exercise. Even though you may think you're wasting more energy, exercise restores levels of serotonin and repairs the damage of burnout.

Don't underestimate the potential damage of burnout. It is the leading cause of depression in America today. Take a hint from me, the original Dr. Burnout, and learn to slow down!

SUMMARY

Depression encourages us to keep to ourselves. It wants us to focus only on our own needs. Believe me, depression's siren call is seductive. There within its dark, quiet environment, it is easy to engage in endless speculation of your own life and its myriad problems. If you succumb too long to depression's seductive emotions, however, you'll find yourself smaller emotionally, less developed as one of God's children, content to live out your life in the frigid, dark waters of a small pond.

Could the above paragraph be talking about you? If so, it's time to break out of

PHYSICIAN'S FACT

1. Burnout is the leading cause of depression in the workforce today.

2. Learning to manage your time and focus your priorities are keys to avoiding burnout.

3. Sleep is absolutely essential and cannot be "made up" for.

4. Get rid of that stinking thinking!

the pond and discover the wonderful depths of the ocean of life. Use the attitude-affirmer "Every day, focus on the needs of others" to grow in God's love. In doing so, you'll discover you're not the only one in this world who needs love, patience, and a kind word. And when you give each of those to someone in need, your heart and spirit will grow deeper, higher, wider, and happier.

DAY 28
Every Day: Give God the Freedom to Use Your Depression for His Glory

The Power to Win

Yes, you read today's attitude-affirmer correctly. And by now maybe you're buying into the concept that God can actually use your depression for his glory. If so, you've made tremendous strides since the beginning of this book, and I want to congratulate you!

God's Word clearly teaches that all things that happen to us can be used ultimately for our good: "We know that all things work together for good for those who love God, who are called according to his purpose" (Rom. 8:28 NRSV). The last time I checked, depression is a part of "all things."

How can your depression be used for something good? There are several ways. Let's begin with your worship of God.

Joni Eareckson Tada, in her beautiful book *When God Weeps*, tells of going to the small church she and her husband attend. One of the families who sits a few rows in front of them has an eleven-year-old girl named Veronica. At first Joni thought the young girl had an inordinate amount of colds and coughs. Then she discovered Veronica was actually fighting cystic fibrosis, a severe lung disease. With CF, the future is not normally long or pain free. Nevertheless, Veronica came to church regularly and did good deeds in the community. Even at her young age, she was able to spearhead a project to collect hundreds of toys for orphaned children in Bosnia.

Joni goes on to say:

I enjoy glancing over at Veronica during worship service. Especially when we sing hymns.

Breathe on me, Breath of God,
Fill me with life anew,
That I may love what Thou dost love,
And do what Thou wouldst do.

She coughs in between the lines and I wonder what God must be thinking as he receives her praise. A genuine sacrifice of praise, it is, as she wheezes through the hymn. Veronica, with her limited lung capacity, inspires me to fill my chest and harmonize with all my heart.

A sacrifice brightens God's glory. It demonstrates the enormously high value we attach to him. Such praise costs us our logic, pride, and preferences. But it's worth it. "Worthy is the Lamb, who was slain, to receive power and wealth and wisdom and strength and honor and glory and praise!" (Revelation 5:12–13).[1]

Whew! That's a powerful thought. But it's taken a lifetime in a wheelchair for Joni to attain wisdom of this sort. And it was only as she gave her problems to God that he has been able to use her paralysis for both her good and his glory. Can we do the same thing with our depression?

Imagine yourself at church this next Sunday. All around you are people with their own problems and trials. But you mainly see them as smiling and confident. In your heart of hearts, it may seem as if they are worthy of God's love; you may believe he wants to receive their worship. But when you look at yourself, an unworthy, guilty person stares back. "How could God love someone like this?" you ask yourself.

It is at this point, however, that a small miracle occurs.

Those around you won't see it. The pastor and choir will never be aware of it. But as you decide to ignore your negative emotions and believe God loves you, and as you lift your heart and soul in praise of his name, I imagine angels in heaven nudging one another to stop and pay attention. All heaven begins to rejoice as, in spite of your depression and poor self-attitude, you worship God. "Worthy is the Lamb!" the celestial inhabitants sing as they join you in honoring the One who can inspire love in the face of depression.

Your fellow members never see it, but God does. He knows the sacrifice you have made to come to church, sit with others in a public place, and worship. In doing so, you have said, "God is more important than my depression. I will praise him regardless of how I feel."

Do you remember the poor widow who put two mites in the temple treasury? Jesus watched this woman stand in line, waiting as the rich threw in a hundred—maybe a thousand—times more than she could ever afford. When it came her turn, she gave what she could to God. Still it was a pitiful amount. Scholars tell us Jesus, in describing this woman, chose the Greek word that meant the poorest of the poor. And yet . . . and yet . . . Jesus said this woman gave more than anyone else!

Learn a lesson from the lips of Christ. The people saw the amount. God saw the love and the sacrifice.

Could it be that when you worship God in spite of your depression, you, of all the other people in the church that day, are actually the one giving the most? God sees your love. And he sees your sacrifice. Remember this when you go to church next Sunday. Even better, remember it every day!

STRENGTH FOR TODAY
Just Barely Going On

In the middle of a busy clinic afternoon, I received a call from the intensive care unit. It seemed my comatose patient had awakened and was standing on the ledge outside his seventh-floor window threatening to jump. As I hurried from the clinic to the hospital, I reviewed the man's case.

He was a prisoner who had ingested three bottles of aspirin in an attempt to kill himself. The ambulance brought him in a comatose state to the intensive care unit and into my care. For three days I had juggled his metabolic status trying to offset the effects of aspirin overdose. Consultation with psychiatry had proven fruitless. They believed he was faking his coma so he wouldn't have to go back to prison.

Now as I hurried through the intensive care unit, I was certain a psychiatrist would take the man's problems seriously. I entered the small alcove where he had spent the past three days in his bed. The patient's hospital gown could be seen blowing in the wind as he stood outside the window. I approached the man slowly, aware that any false move might provoke him. I leaned out the window where I could make eye contact with him. The building stretched seven stories to the ground, and I felt dizzy and panicky. I tried to ignore the feeling and concentrate on my patient. After several minutes of unconvincing conversation, I realized I was getting nowhere. He turned his anguished eyes on me and shouted.

"I just can't go on! I don't want to go back to prison. I've got nothing to live for."

Suicide is a difficult topic to address. The fear of suggesting suicide to a depressed individual prevents discussion of the possibility. Yet studies have shown such discussions do not induce suicide but rather open doorways of communication.

Comfort can be taken from the fact that not everyone who thinks about suicide actually attempts it. But thoughts of suicide are a warning sign. If you or someone you know has such thoughts, treatment is mandatory. Act quickly.

What are the warning signs of suicide? "Winding up one's affairs" should be taken as a serious move toward ending one's life. Also, rehearsing a suicide or seriously discussing one or more specific methods should

> ## Tools for Tomorrow
>
> ### LIFEFILTER 28
>
> *Letting My Weaknesses Become My Strengths*
> "We know that all things work together for good for those who love God, who are called according to his purpose" (Rom. 8:28, NRSV).
>
> #### TODAY
> 1. I will plan to go to church this Sunday and worship God, my Lord and Savior.
> 2. I will ask God to help me use this depression for his glory.
> 3. I will never give up on life because God's love never gives up on me!

sound an alarm. Increased use of drugs or alcohol may precede an attempt. Most dangerously, depressed individuals seeming to have passed the worst point and on the road to apparent recovery discover the energy to attempt suicide.

- One way to handle these thoughts is to contract with a friend or counselor that you will not attempt anything without first letting him or her know.
- In fact, making a contract with one's self is helpful. At the top of a sheet of paper, write down three friends or associates and their phone numbers who can be contacted in the event of thoughts of suicide.
- Beneath that, list at least three warning signs from personal experience that lead to such thoughts.
- Next outline at least four or five responses that can be shared with a friend who is considering suicide. These thoughts can then be applied personally.
- Finally, make an activity list of things to do in the event of suicidal thoughts, such as:

  1. Contact doctor.
  2. Contact friends or family.
  3. Throw away alcohol and unnecessary medications.
  4. Prepare for possible hospitalization (if doctor advises).
  5. Read spiritual journal entries.
  6. Don't let depression win.

Is there hope? Is there something worth living for? You bet! The fact that I am writing this book says there is a role for someone who has been depressed in helping others.

Oh, yes! You may be wondering what happened to my patient.

I looked him in the eyes and said, "You may not have a reason to live, but there are others like you who must be stopped from committing crimes. If you feel your life has any purpose left, think about those prisoners like yourself. Maybe you can help them so that other victims will not suffer. Make your life count for something good. Don't end it this way."

Surprisingly, the man reached out and took my hand. He came back in the window and was admitted to the psychiatric ward. Months later I received a letter from him. He had become a Christian and was involved in prison ministry helping criminals with their rehabilitation. He realized he would never go home again, but he had made his life count for something positive.

There is always something to live for!

SUMMARY

Those around you won't see it. The pastor and choir will never be aware of it. But as you decide to ignore your negative emotions and believe God loves you and as you lift your heart and soul in praise of his name, I imagine angels in heaven nudging one another to stop and pay attention. All heaven begins to rejoice as, in spite of your depression and poor self-attitude, you worship God. "Worthy is the Lamb!" the celestial inhabitants sing as they join you in honoring the One who can inspire love in the face of depression.

Your fellow members never see it, but God does. He knows the sacrifice you have made to come to church, sit with others in a public place, and worship. In doing so, you have said, "God is more important than my depression. I will praise him regardless of how I feel."

> ### PHYSICIAN'S FACT
>
> 1. Suicidal thoughts are a common part of depression.
> 2. Be aware of the warning signs of suicidal intent.
> 3. Make a pact with friends or family.
> 4. Make a checklist to help you think clearly about such thoughts.
> 5. Remember, there is always something good to live for!

Could it be that when you worship God in spite of your depression you, of all the other people in the church on that day, are actually the one giving the most? God sees your love. And he sees your sacrifice.

Remember this when you go to church next Sunday. Even better, remember it every day.

DAY 29
Use Your Depression to Help Others

THE POWER TO WIN

It's time to embrace your depression.

What are you talking about, Mark? I'd rather hug a porcupine. Do you know what this disease has done to me? Can you understand the emotional pain and suffering I've endured because of it? And now you want me to "embrace it"?

I don't want you to do this. God does.

Do you remember Paul? The first missionary of the New Testament church and the most prolific of all the New Testament writers, this man had to learn to embrace his weakness. "To keep me from becoming conceited because of these surpassingly great revelations, there was given me a thorn in my flesh, a messenger of Satan, to torment me. Three times I pleaded with the Lord to take it away from me. But he said to me, 'My grace is sufficient for you, for my power is made perfect in weakness.' Therefore I will boast all the more gladly about my weaknesses, so that Christ's power may rest on me" (2 Cor. 12:7–9).

We really don't know what Paul's "thorn in the flesh" consisted of. Some have theorized it was a disease of the eyes. Others believe he had a speech impediment. In any case, grab hold of this thought and let it take root in your heart: it was God's will that this "messenger from Satan" be a part of Paul's daily life!

Why would God do this? There are two reasons: First, it was a "blessing in disguise" for Paul. He had to learn both to live with this problem and to continue loving God at the same time. Doing this daily taught Paul the absolute necessity of leaning completely on his heavenly Father for daily support. His native intelligence couldn't overcome this "thorn in the flesh." A powerful personality and incredible capacity for work helped him not at all in this area of his life. Only an utter dependence on God could make a difference. Second, God received praise from others as they realized how Paul could be a powerful witness for Christ and still have these problems. The bottom line was that this problem took everyone's attention off of Paul and put it on God, where it belonged.

> Ask yourself this question: Why has God chosen to let me suffer from depression? Believe me, it's not to make you feel guilty but to help you do good.

Wouldn't it be interesting if Paul's "thorn in the flesh" had been depression! I believe that Paul, as an artist and scholar, could have easily suffered from this problem. In any case, perhaps God has allowed you and me to fight the same battle as the apostle for the same reasons: He wants us to learn more of him and to rely completely upon him. God wants us to be witnesses of his power to others who suffer from a number of different problems.

Another question: Could Satan, knowing the power of Christians who live triumphant lives through giving their weaknesses to God, try to keep those same believers apart from the world? Could Satan tempt us to want to be isolated, knowing that if we began to live for Christ by letting him use our depression we would become some of God's most effective witnesses? If this is true (and I believe it is), then it behooves us to rise up against the emotions of depression and get out into the world where we can be a positive example to others who need help.

"My power is made perfect in weakness." Those words allow you and me to see depression in a different light. We don't have to like our depression. Paul didn't want his "thorn in the flesh." But if we can ever get to the point where we quit giving up and feeling sorry for ourselves, we place our lives on an entirely different path. And if we can give our depression to God and ask him to use it for his glory, something wonderful happens, both to others and to ourselves.

Ask yourself this question: Why has God chosen to let me suffer from depression? Believe me, it's not to make you feel guilty but to help you do good.

She was timid, scared, and suicidal. As the young woman sat in my office, she admitted to a childhood filled with abuse. Abuse that had scarred her memories and wounded her soul. Abuse that had left her depressed and consumed with guilt. Now she wanted to die.

Several days before she had been driving in her car, contemplating how to end it all. As she turned on the radio, Jane just "happened" to hear one of my sixty-second radio spots. In that one minute God reached out and touched her heart. The flicker of hope began to build in her, and Sunday found her in our church hanging on every word of the sermon.

Now, in my office, she had retreated into a shell and talked again of suicide.

Person after person had tried to help her. Because of the memories of abuse, however, she was unable to let them get close to her emotionally. To make things worse, here I was, a male, sitting across from her in a small office. I could almost see the fear beating at her, telling her to get out of the office before something bad happened—like when she was a child.

"Jane, I know a little of what you're going through because I also suffer from depression," I said.

"You!" She didn't believe me. "You get up and speak in front of thousands of people. You smile and help people all around you. How can you possibly know what it's like to be depressed?"

I began telling her about the sometimes daily battles I have with depression. I shared how insecure and guilty it tried to make me feel. When I told her of how there were days I didn't want to get out of bed, much less see people, she nodded her head. But it was as I admitted that I had to work very hard sometimes to believe God loved me as much as he loved others that I finally began to see her relax.

"How can you preach and counsel if you fight depression?" she wanted to know. I told her about some of the ways I've learned to trust in God in spite of my emotions. I explained how I've decided to believe God's Word more than I trust my emotions. And I told her of the wonderful times I've had with the Lord, even deep in depression, when I've continued to pray and read my Bible.

"Could I learn to do that?" she asked hopefully.

Not only could she; today this young woman is a living testimony to the power of God in overcoming years of abuse and depression. She is using her weaknesses to help others who have not yet discovered God loves them and wants, through Jesus Christ, to give them a wonderful life.

Could I have ever reached this woman without having fought depression? I don't think so. By admitting my depression and sharing both the problems I've had and the victories I've won, God was able to use my weakness for his glory. To put it another way: a life was saved because I fight depression!

How can God use your depression? Who is waiting in the wings, lonely and confused, for a sensitive word from you? Believe me, people who need your help are all around. And as you show how you can identify through their depression, God begins both to perfect you and to strengthen them.

STRENGTH FOR TODAY
Surprise, Surprise

Mark Sutton approached me about helping to write this book when I was in a happy time of my life. Up to that point I had suffered from previous bouts of mild to major depression in my twenties and thirties, but I was nearing my fortieth birthday in relatively good spirits. After I agreed to help Mark, my life took a drastic downward turn. I have already detailed some of the events that plunged me into a major depression.

I do not think it is a coincidence Mark asked me to help him. God knew the path I was to walk as I prepared to write this book. God knew my experiences would be difficult but that I would eventually triumph with his help. God knew I would gain wisdom to share with you as you read this book. Please do not let my struggles go to waste. Learn from them.

During the course of this book, I've advised you to seek professional counseling. I have been there and benefited enormously from it. But what about the rest of my advice? Did I do everything I have asked you to do? Yes!

As I began to write this book in earnest, the realization came to me that I had been through a difficult but rewarding task—professional counseling. An extended period of intense personal inspection was painful but ultimately rewarding. Then, although I had fine-tuned my emotional, psychological, and spiritual life, I had not paid attention to my physical condition. I took the advice I've given you.

I had noticed an uncomfortable burning in my throat when I walked up two flights of stairs. I denied it for months, but the possibility of heart disease continued to nag at me. In October I relented and made an appointment with my doctor. After all, I had only seen him a few months earlier, hadn't I? I was to find out it had been four years since I had last seen the doctor!

My first brush with reality came when I stepped on the scales. I weighed a whopping 265 pounds! This couldn't be! The last time I had weighed I had been a slightly chubby 210. When did I gain 55 pounds? The next shock came when the doctor checked my blood pressure. I almost blew the mercury out of the gauge through the examining room ceiling!

Tools for Tomorrow

LifeFilter 29

Trust in God's Grace, No Matter What

"To keep me from becoming conceited because of these surpassingly great revelations, there was given me a thorn in my flesh, a messenger of Satan, to torment me. Three times I pleaded with the Lord to take it away from me. But he said to me, 'My grace is sufficient for you, for my power is made perfect in weakness.' Therefore I will boast all the more gladly about my weaknesses, so that Christ's power may rest on me" (2 Cor. 12:7–9).

Today

1. God can use even my depression for his glory.
2. I will seek ways to use my depression for God and not let depression use me.
3. I will make my own plan, using the suggestions from *Conquering Depression*, to overcome depression.

What followed was a disturbing barrage of facts and figures such as cholesterol level, EKG changes, and triglyceride levels until I was lost in a depressive blur of information. An hour later I sat in my doctor's office and waited for the bad news. He was kind and understanding, but he stated one chilling fact: "You know what you have to do."

Yes, I knew what I had to do. I had told patients in the past what they had to do. Now it was time for me to swallow my own medicine. Fortunately a stress test revealed I had no heart disease. But I had to get the weight down and start on an exercise program. The program I chose was *SugarBusters,* a popular weight-loss program currently enjoying great success.

I joined the hospital fitness center and began a simple program of walking every day. Not running, just walking. I had a bad back, and I was afraid that if I started running again I would suffer back pain. I began with half a mile a day and eventually worked up to three miles a day. I chose to use my time of walking as an opportunity to talk to God. This special time of the day became sacred to me, and I eagerly anticipated the walks.

My friends and family told me I was crazy to try to lose weight over the Thanksgiving and Christmas holidays. Wait until the new year, they told me. But I decided that if I could lose weight during the tastiest months of the year I could lose weight anytime! By Christmas I had lost twenty-five pounds! What a nice present to give myself.

As I write these last few chapters, I can safely state that I have done all that I advised you to do. Through my diet I have lost more than sixty pounds. I am continuing my daily exercise, and my spirits have soared. My cholesterol and triglyceride levels have plummeted. I am in the best physical shape I have been in for years. And most importantly, depression comes infrequently and stays shorter than one night. I have never felt better in my life!

You can do it! I know because I did it.

I have walked where you are walking. I have struggled where you are struggling. I have the victory in my life over depression by following the simple health guidelines in this book. You can do it too! And having achieved a healthy lifestyle, I can testify that it definitely helps keep depression at bay. Try it and succeed!

SUMMARY

"My power is made perfect in weakness." Those words allow you and me to see depression in a different light. We don't have to like our depression; Paul didn't want his "thorn in the flesh." But if we can ever get to the point where we quit giving up and feeling sorry for ourselves, we place our lives on an entirely different path. And if we can give our depression to God and ask him to use it for his glory, something wonderful happens—both to others and to ourselves.

How can God use your depression? Who is waiting in the wings, lonely and confused, for a sensitive word from you? People who need your help are all around. And as you show how you can identify through their depression, God begins both to perfect you and strengthen them.

> **PHYSICIAN'S FACT**
>
> 1. Victory can be yours with God's help.
> 2. Using suggestions from this book, create your own plan to conquer depression.
> 3. Be patient and persistent, and you will ultimately triumph.

DAY 30
Let This Book Help You Forever

The Power to Win

Congratulations! You've made it to the last chapter, the last day! But where do you go from here?

A more correct question would be, where do we go from here? If you flip back to the beginning of the book, you'll find our promising to help you put together a team that will stay with you the rest of your life. So, if you don't mind, we'd like to continue to be a part of your everyday life.

How can we do this? The following are some suggestions and hints to help you continue defeating depression and discovering joy:

- *Read the book again!* Did you absorb and master every concept of every chapter? You don't have to spend as much time on every chapter as before, but I guarantee reading *Conquering Depression* a second time will help you discover things in the book you missed the first time.

- *Recommend the book to a friend who might need it.* Am I suggesting this so we can sell another copy? Sure! No, the truth is that Bruce and I believe deeply in God's power to use this book in the lives of those who are depressed. But the overall reason I want you to share knowledge of this book with someone else is that it will give you something positive to discuss with a friend. And in talking about your depression, you begin to lessen its power. In listening to the problems of your friend, you may be able to help them out of the dark pit that overwhelms them.

- *Continue to use your LifeFilters.* If you haven't laminated them, I encourage you to do so. Carry one of them with you every day for the foreseeable future. Perhaps three or four of them touch especially sensitive areas of your life. If so, you might want to keep one of these, in addition to the regular rotation of LifeFilters, always with you.
- *Read your Bible every day.* It is absolutely imperative that you feed yourself spiritually every day. The health of your soul depends on your doing this.
- *Pray without ceasing.* Actually the apostle Paul said this a long time before I thought of it. But the advice is still good. I have gotten in the habit of lifting what I call "little prayers" up to God forty or fifty times a day. On the way to work I pray for every member of my family. In the first minutes of getting to my office, I ask God for his wisdom and protection through the day. And about once an hour, I thank God for his love. I think Paul knew this kind of attitude keeps us focused on God even while living in and dealing with this world.
- *Attend church regularly.* Don't let anything or anyone drive you away from your church. Don't let any emotion have control over your church attendance. If you haven't yet done so, find a church where the Bible is accepted as authoritative for all aspects of life, and where the pastor applies it to *your* life.
- *Follow the doctor's instructions.* Bruce has some wonderful prescriptions in the next section for overcoming depression. Follow them faithfully!
- *Know that I am praying for you every day.* If you are holding this book and reading these words, then I am praying for you. In fact, I have prayed for you every day as I've written this book. Before you ever picked it up, I prayed that God would lead you to find this book and read it. As you've gone through the chapters, I've prayed God would give you the strength to follow these instructions and conquer depression. And now that you've finished the book, know that neither God nor I are finished with you. He will always love you and be there for you. I have covenanted with God to pray every day for you.

- *Write to me.* If this book has blessed you or if you have a special prayer request, I invite you to E-mail me at *Mark_Sutton@msn.com.* I don't guarantee I can answer every E-mail personally, but I do promise to read every letter and pray for every need.

Let me close with a story about you.

Many years ago in India, a water carrier trudged from his home to the river every day. There he would fill two huge clay pots with water and then put them on his shoulders, a stout pole holding them in place. He would then return to his home and use the water in his daily tasks.

One of the pots was always sad during the return trip. This is because small fissures ran across its surface, allowing water to leak out. By the time its master had gotten to his home, fully half of the pot's water was gone. Because it loved the master, this pot felt guilty for being such a poor container.

One day the pot got up enough courage to speak to its master. "Oh sir," it said, "I am so sorry to cause you so much trouble."

"What are you talking about?" asked the master.

The pot was ashamed. "Because I am such a poor container, I waste the precious water you gather. The cracks in my surface make me unworthy to help you anymore. I wish to be thrown away."

Smiling gently, the master said, "You have completely misunderstood. There are other pots without cracks I could be using. You have seen them by the side of the house. Haven't you ever wondered why I insist on using you instead of them?"

The pot had to admit it had often wondered this very thing.

"It's because you can do something for me none of the others can do."

"Me?" The clay pot was incredulous. "I have cracks and fissures that make me weak. How is this possible?"

"I am the master," the man replied. "I see and plan things you do not begin to understand. But this once, I will show you how you are uniquely valuable to me." And picking up the cracked clay pot, he began walking toward the river.

"Do you see how beautiful the flowers are on this road?"

The pot nodded with wonder. It had never really noticed the beauty evident on the journey to and from the river. Instead, it had always focused on its weaknesses.

"After filling you each day, I always make sure to put you on the shoulder closest to the side of the road. As I walk, your cracks and fissures allow the water to trickle out and nourish the soil between the river and our home. As a result, this portion of the land is more beautiful than any other."

The pot was stunned. "Do you mean to say I have had a part in bringing about this beauty?"

The master nodded. "It is *only* because of your system of cracks and fissures that these flowers have been able to bloom. Your weaknesses, given to me, have become your strengths. Through them, together we have created wondrous beauty."

You, fellow struggler, are the cracked clay pot. Not a crackpot, mind you! But a vessel lined with cracks and fissures. Perhaps you feel your depression makes you a poor container for God's love.

Focus upon your weaknesses, and you'll never see the beauty in life's journey. Place too much guilt upon yourself, and you'll never notice how God wants to use you.

But if you will give your depression to God and allow him to use you—weaknesses and all—then he will begin to show how his strength is made perfect in your weakness. He'll draw your attention to the lives touched by your compassion and sensitivity. Your heavenly Father, who loves you so deeply he allowed his only Son to die for you, will take your weaknesses and, out of them, create works of wondrous beauty. Realize your depression just might be the best tool God has to do some great things and touch some needy lives. Thank him for using you for his glory. And one more thing. Look up and enjoy the journey.

"Keep yourselves in God's love as you wait for the mercy of our Lord Jesus Christ to bring you to eternal life. Be merciful to those who doubt. . . . To him who is able to keep you from falling and to present you before his glorious presence without fault and with great joy—to the only God our Savior be glory, majesty, power and authority, through Jesus Christ our Lord, before all ages, now and forevermore! Amen" (Jude 21–22, 24–25).

— MARK

STRENGTH FOR TODAY
From Here to Where?

We have finally come to the end of thirty days. I certainly hope you have learned something. I have not covered all of the in-depth information there is about depression. In fact, I have only exposed the tip of the iceberg. I have listed in the back of this book Internet sights you can consult for more information about depression. Also see the notes section for helpful books and articles.

Don't be afraid to question and learn. It will keep your mind prepared for the attack of the beast of depression. As I write these final words, I would like to share with you my formula for continued success. I developed an approach to depression during my counseling that has helped me recognize and stave off depression's advances. Coupled with my eating habits and daily exercise, this formula has kept me free from major depression for three years.

• *Keep that spiritual journal.* Use it to talk about how you feel when you are down, and then write something positive and uplifting, such as a simple blessing God has shown you through the trials of your day. Most importantly, keep the journal readily available. When I feel the cold claws of depression, I pick up my journal and look back through my past to a time when I felt worse than I currently do. It is amazing to see how depressed I was; but it is even more thrilling to see how God worked me through it. Reviewing past victories can give you hope to conquer your current crisis.

• *Read the Bible daily.* I am continually surprised how God can say so much through the same verse I have read many times before. Reading the Bible is more than reviewing literature. It is a face-to-face encounter with God. I remember this as I open the Book. God is about to speak to me through his Word! When I begin to get depressed, I ask, "Have you been reading your Bible lately?" Always the answer is no. We are composed of body, mind, and soul. Do not forsake the nourishment of your soul. It is even more important than the nourishment of your body.

• *Talk to God.* People who see me driving down the road think I am insane. When I am alone in my car, I constantly talk to God. I imagine Jesus sitting in the passenger seat, and I carry on a conversation with him. A few years ago I even wrote a play about a man who tries to introduce all of his friends to an imaginary person, Jesus. Although the effect was comical, it raised the question of how we would act if we had Jesus with us all the time. In fact, this situation is not fictional. If you are a Christian, Jesus is with you all the time. Stop and talk to him from time to time. You'll find the conversations enlightening. And you may find some answers!

• *Check your spiritual compass.* I devised a compass to help me determine in which direction my life was pointed. At one point of the compass was God, his work and will for my life, and the concept of a God-centered existence. At the south pole and opposite end were my selfish desires, my unreasonable dreams, my "Bruce-centered" life. I made a list of those things I desired that were God-centered at the north pole and those things in my life that were Bruce-centered at the south pole. Whenever I would begin to feel depressed, I would check my compass and find I was wandering south—off of the path God wants me to walk. I would have to turn myself around toward

---

Tools for Tomorrow

LifeFilter 30

Congratulations Are in Order!

"To him who is able to keep you from falling and to present you before his glorious presence without fault and with great joy—to the only God our Savior be glory, majesty, power and authority, through Jesus Christ our Lord, before all ages, now and forevermore! Amen" (Jude 24–25).

Today

1. Congratulations! I've made it through the entire book!

2. Congratulations! God loves me, Jesus lives in me, and my future is going to be wonderful as his Spirit guides me.

3. Congratulations! I'm going to relax in God's love and enjoy the journey, no matter what my emotional outlook may be at the time.

the north pole. Toward God. Toward God-centeredness. By doing so, I would turn away from the path leading to depression and back toward the pathway of joy.

• *Be consistent.* I have to constantly stop and read this checklist. I ask myself: How am I doing? Am I drifting away from the proper course? Am I eating properly and exercising? Am I doing the things listed above? Just as you must go to your doctor for frequent checkups, you must go to the Great Physician for frequent checkups. Do so and you will remain consistent.

• *Consult your LifeFilters daily.* Every day, I pick a LifeFilter card at random and carry it with me. Throughout the day when I feel the fingers of depression crawling up my neck, I pull out the LifeFilter and review the Bible verse and the key concepts for that day. God always seems to guide me to the LifeFilter I need for that day. Give it a try!

I hope you will find help in these suggestions. Make up your own list of crucial aids. The important ingredients to victory are knowledge and having a plan. Through this book I hope I have given you the tools you can use to devise your own plan.

May God bless you!

— BRUCE

SUMMARY

If you will give your depression to God and allow him to use you—weaknesses and all—he will begin to show how his strength is made perfect in your weakness. He'll draw your attention to the lives touched by your compassion and sensitivity. Your heavenly Father, who loves you so deeply he allowed his only Son to die for you, will take your weaknesses and, out of them, create works of wondrous beauty.

Realize that your depression just might be the best tool God has to do some great things and touch some needy lives. Thank him for using you for his glory. And, one more thing.

Look up and enjoy the journey!

INTERNET SOURCES

1. www.depression.com
2. www.depression-net.com
3. www.psycom.net/depression.central.html
4. www.teachhealth.com (This is an online book about stress by a Christian physician.)

NOTES

Day 3

1. Charles Stanley, *How to Handle Adversity* (Nashville: Oliver-Nelson Books, 1989), 101.

Day 6

1. *Editor's Clip Sheets*, December 1993, 3.

Day 7

1. *Proclaim*, October-December 1992.

Day 8

1. Mark S. Gold, *The Good News about Depression* (New York: Bantam Books, 1995), 170.

Day 14

1. Medard Laz, *Love Adds a Little Chocolate* (New York: Warner Books, 1997), 85.

Day 15

1. Joseph R. Dunn, "Medical Perspectives on Humor: An Interview with William F. Fry, M.D.," *Humor and Health Journal*, 2.1 (January/February 1993).

Day 16

1. David T. McClellan, *Homiletics*, May 1998, 36.

2. John L. Mason, *An Enemy Called Average* (Tulsa: John L. Mason, 1990), 49.

3. Carol Hart, *Secrets of Serotonin* (Boston: St. Martin's Press, 1996), 25.

Day 18

1. John C. Maxwell, *The Success Journey* (Nashville: Thomas Nelson Publishers, 1997), 155–56.

Day 25

1. Alice Grey, *Stories for the Heart* (Sisters, Oreg.: Multnomah Books, 1996), 88.

2. Barbara Johnson, *Mama, Get the Hammer, There's a Fly on Papa's Head!* (Dallas: Word Publishing, 1994), 95.

3. Ellen McGrath, Ph.D., *Beating the Blues* (New York: Macmillan Publishing, 1998), 53–66.

4. Brian P. Quinn, Ph.D., *The Depression Sourcebook* (Los Angeles: Lowell House, 1998), 27–37.

Introduction to Part 6

1. Walter Wangerin Jr., *Mourning into Dancing* (Grand Rapids, Mich.: Zondervan Publishing House, 1992), 266–68.

Day 27

1. Cal and Roae Samra, *More Holy Humor* (Carmel, N.Y.: Guideposts, 1997), 139.

2. Billy Graham, *Unto the Hills* (Dallas: Word Publishing, 1996), 53.

Day 28

1. Joni Eareckson Tada, *When God Weeps* (Grand Rapids, Mich.: Zondervan Publishing, 1997), 109–10.

LifeFilter 1
How to Develop a Battle Plan

"If God is for us, who can be against us? He who did not spare his own Son, but gave him up for us all—how will he not also, along with him, graciously give us all things?" (Rom. 8:31b–32).

LifeFilter 2
How to Have Peace Today

"And the peace of God, which transcends all understanding, will guard your hearts and your minds in Christ Jesus" (Phil 4:7).

LifeFilter 3
How to Use Depression Before It Uses Me

"But he said to me, 'My grace is sufficient for you, for my power is made perfect in weakness.' Therefore I will boast all the more gladly about my weaknesses, so that Christ's power may rest on me. . . For when I am weak, then I am strong" (2 Cor.

LifeFilter 4
How to Reject the Guilt and Embrace the Cure

"The sun shall not strike you by day,
Nor the moon by night.
The LORD shall preserve you from all evil;
He shall preserve your soul" (Ps. 121:6–7 NKJV).

TODAY

1. Remember: I'm not alone; God is with me.
2. Keep my eyes on God, not on the circumstances surrounding me.
3. God's power can change the situation when he thinks it's time.
4. My heavenly Father will take care of me—no matter what!

TODAY
I will . . .

1. Get rid of the guilt trip and focus on the cure.
2. Recognize that depression is an illness that can have a physical basis.
3. Remember that God's Word, not my present emotional outlook, is my authority.

TODAY

1. God loves me. And that's why I can win the battle against depression, because I've got God on my side.
2. Remember: God is greater than my depression.
3. Believe: God loves me, regardless of my emotional outlook!

TODAY
I will use stress in a positive way to:

1. Examine my relationship with God.
2. Be a reminder to pray.
3. Help me grow stronger psychologically and spiritually.

LifeFilter 5
Physical and Spiritual Attitude Check

"Those who hope in the LORD will renew their strength. They will soar on wings like eagles; they will run and not grow weary, they will walk and not be faint" (Isa. 40:31).

LifeFilter 6
How to Make My Life's Foundation Strong and Sure

Jesus says, "I stand at the door and knock. If anyone hears my voice and opens the door, I will come in" (Rev. 3:20).

LifeFilter 7
Take a Well-Deserved Rest!

"Come to me, all you who are weary and burdened, and I will give you rest" (Matt. 11:28).

LifeFilter 8
The Keys to a Great Future

"Brothers, I do not consider myself yet to have taken hold of it. But one thing I do: Forgetting what is behind and straining toward what is ahead, I press on toward the goal to win the prize for which God has called me heavenward in Christ Jesus" (Phil. 3:13–14).

TODAY
I will give Jesus Christ . . .

1. All my fears.
2. All my guilt.
3. All my mistakes.
4. Control of my life.

TODAY

1. I will remember always to trust in God, no matter what my emotional state may be at the moment.
2. I will begin looking for someone who can help with my depression.
3. I will *not* give up!

TODAY
Have I . . .

1. Had a physician check my physical condition?
2. Tried to take God's view of my situation?
3. Promised God to endure no matter what?

TODAY
Remember to . . .

1. Put aside the distractions of life.
2. Ignore the worries that sap my energy and time.
3. Focus on my Heavenly Father.
4. Believe that God loves me, even with my faults and weaknesses.

LifeFilter 9
Crossing the Chasm
from Fear to Faith

"So do not fear, for I am with you;
do not be dismayed, for I am your God.
I will strengthen you and help you;
I will uphold you with my righteous right hand"
(Isa. 41:10).

LifeFilter 10
Trusting God and Helping Others

"I will say of the LORD, 'He is my refuge
and my fortress,
my God, in whom I trust'" (Ps. 91:2).

LifeFilter 11
Reviewing My "Fantastic Voyage"

"The LORD is my light and my salvation—
whom shall I fear?
The LORD is the stronghold of my life—
of whom shall I be afraid?" (Ps. 27:1).

LifeFilter 12
The Medicine of Divine Love

"The LORD your God is with you,
he is mighty to save.
He will take great delight in you,
he will quiet you with his love,
he will rejoice over you with singing" (Zeph. 3:17).

TODAY

1. I will look for someone to help.
2. I will begin to look for a Christian physician to partner with me in overcoming depression.
3. I will thank God for loving me and being my constant partner.

TODAY

1. I will thank God for providing both spiritual and physical medicines that can help me.
2. I will establish and maintain a daily quiet time.
3. Right now I will stop and thank God for loving me.

TODAY

1. I refuse to let the fear of depression terrorize me anymore.
2. There are physical and emotional reasons for my depression that can—and will—be overcome.
3. I will be patient as the repair work is being completed.

TODAY

1. God's light of love is shining upon me.
2. Review the progress I've made since beginning *Conquering Depression*.
3. God is carrying me close to his heart on this "fantastic voyage" called life.

LifeFilter 13
Studying God's Word and Medicine's Laws

"Do not let this Book of the Law depart from your mouth; meditate on it day and night, so that you may be careful to do everything written in it. Then you will be prosperous and successful" (Josh. 1:8).

LifeFilter 14
Understanding God Cares for Me

"Cast all your anxiety on him because he cares for you" (1 Pet. 5:7).

LifeFilter 15
A Cheerful Heart Is Good Medicine

"If you obey my commands, you will remain in my love. . . . I have told you this so that my joy may be in you and that your joy may be complete" (John 15:10a,11).

LifeFilter 16
A "Touch" of God's Love

"'Lord, if you are willing, you can make me clean.' Jesus reached out his hand and touched the man. 'I am willing,' he said. 'Be clean!'" (Luke 5:12b–13a).

TODAY
I will remember . . .

1. No matter what I face, God cares for *me!*
2. God also cares for me through the concern and wisdom of other Christians.
3. In other words, I am not alone!

TODAY

1. I will partner with God to study his Word on a daily basis.
2. I will partner with my physician to study the treatment options God has provided for my emotional health.
3. I will take a moment to stop and thank God for his love.

TODAY

1. I will thank God for reaching out and touching me through his Son.
2. I will pass on his love by hugging three people.
3. No matter what my emotions tell me, I will remember that God loves me.

TODAY
I will try to . . .

1. Remember, a giggle a day keeps the doctor away. But it also allows the Great Physician to make house calls!
2. Be joyful because God loves me.
3. Smile at five people, and let God's joy flow through me.

LifeFilter 18
Keep on Standing

"Therefore put on the full armor of God, so that when the day of evil comes, you may be able to stand your ground, and after you have done everything, to stand" (Eph. 6:13).

LifeFilter 20
Setting Positive "Stones" in My Life

"But one thing I do: Forgetting what is behind and straining toward what is ahead, I press on toward the goal to win the prize for which God has called me heavenward in Christ Jesus" (Phil. 3:13–14).

LifeFilter 17
Using Communication as a Cure

"Trust in him at all times . . . pour out your hearts to him, for God is our refuge" (Ps. 62:8).

LifeFilter 19
Know the Power of "No!"

"If any of you lacks wisdom, he should ask God, who gives generously to all without finding fault, and it will be given to him" (James 1:5).

TODAY

1. I will rest in the fact that God will *never* give up on me.
2. I resolve to fight my depression and not give up!
3. I will remember God has a special place in his heart for those who endure.

TODAY

1. I will make a list of attainable goals I can work toward that will help me conquer depression.
2. Remember: if I'm having sleep problems, read again and follow Dr. Hennigan's suggestions for sleeping better.
3. Confirm that the stones (goals) in my life are moving me forward in a positive way.
4. I will praise God for helping me move toward a wonderful future.

TODAY

1. I will communicate with God and believe that he hears me.
2. I will open lines of communication through meaningful dialogue with others.
3. I will communicate with my soul by reading and meditating on God's Word.

TODAY

1. Remember that filling others' needs is not a substitute for doing God's will in my life.
2. I will say no to requests I believe are inappropriate.
3. Now that I know the different types of depression, I will examine my emotions to see if they are being influenced by this disease.

LifeFilter 21
My Guide to Restoration after Failure

"So he got up and went to his father. But while he was still a long way off, his father saw him and was filled with compassion for him; he ran to his son, threw his arms around him and kissed him" (Luke 15:20).

LifeFilter 22
I Can Dilute My Depression through Sharing

"Where there is no counsel, the people fall; but in the multitude of counselors there is safety" (Prov. 11:14 NKJV).

LifeFilter 23
Honoring God with My Body

"Do you not know that your body is a temple of the Holy Spirit, who is in you, whom you have received from God? You are not your own; you were bought at a price. Therefore honor God with your body" (1 Cor. 6:19–20).

LifeFilter 24
Making the Best Use of My Time

"Turn my eyes away from worthless things; preserve my life according to your word" (Ps. 119:37).

TODAY

1. Remember: God does not want me to be alone in this world. That's why he is always with me.
2. I resolve to leave isolation and share meaningfully with some positive, wise Christians.
3. If necessary, I will find a godly counselor and let him/her partner with me in overcoming my depression.

TODAY

1. I will remember that God loves me even when I fail.
2. I will believe that my heavenly Father is always waiting, with open arms, to take me back.
3. I will repent of what I've done and ask God's forgiveness.
4. I will begin a daily spiritual H&P. I will write in a journal containing a daily devotion. It's good preventive medicine.

TODAY
I will . . .

1. Look carefully at my habits and give up any that are not God honoring.
2. Identify and remove time wasters that keep me from having a good outlook on life.
3. Feel better by eating better (and healthier).

TODAY

1. Weather permitting, I will get outside and enjoy the sunshine God made for me.
2. I resolve to begin (or continue) a regular program of exercise.
3. I will stop and thank God for sending his Son, Jesus Christ, to forgive my sins and live with me forever.

LifeFilter 26
Believe in God's Love

"For I am convinced that neither death nor life, neither angels nor demons, neither the present nor the future, nor any powers, neither height nor depth, nor anything else in all creation, will be able to separate us from the love of God that is in Christ Jesus our Lord" (Rom. 8:38–39).

LifeFilter 28
Letting My Weaknesses Become My Strengths

"We know that all things work together for good for those who love God, who are called according to his purpose" (Rom. 8:28, NRSV).

LifeFilter 25
Forgiveness: Accepting It and Giving It

"I, even I, am he who blots out your transgressions, for my own sake, and remembers your sins no more" (Isa. 43:25).

LifeFilter 27
Looking Beyond My Own Needs

"Carry each other's burdens, and in this way you will fulfill the law of Christ" (Gal. 6:2).

TODAY

1. Remember that God loves *me!*
2. Take a moment to thank God for his love and for his salvation.
3. Use PEACE (day 26) to find peace while over-coming depression.

TODAY

1. I will plan to go to church this Sunday and wor-ship God, my Lord and Savior.
2. I will ask God to help me use this depression for his glory.
3. I will never give up on life because God's love never gives up on me!

TODAY

1. Believe: that when I ask God, in Jesus Christ, to forgive my sins, he will do it!
2. Let go of guilt and anger.
3. Forgive anyone who has wronged me. I will ask God to help me forgive.
4. Go outside: let God's sun and God's Son warm my life.

TODAY
I will . . .

1. Thank God for meeting my needs.
2. Look for an opportunity to help other people.
3. Identify the activities and thought patterns causing stress in my life and try to change them.

LifeFilter 29
Trust in God's Grace, No Matter What

"To keep me from becoming conceited because of these surpassingly great revelations, there was given me a thorn in my flesh, a messenger of Satan, to torment me. Three times I pleaded with the Lord to take it away from me. But he said to me, 'My grace is sufficient for you, for my power is made perfect in weakness.' Therefore I will boast all the more gladly about my weaknesses, so that Christ's power may rest on me"

LifeFilter 30
Congratulations Are in Order!

"To him who is able to keep you from falling and to present you before his glorious presence without fault and with great joy—to the only God our Savior be glory, majesty, power and authority, through Jesus Christ our Lord, before all ages, now and forevermore! Amen" (Jude 24–25).

TODAY

1. Congratulations! I've made it through the entire book!

2. Congratulations! God loves me, Jesus lives in me, and my future is going to be wonderful as his Spirit guides me.

3. Congratulations! I'm going to relax in God's love and enjoy the journey, no matter what my emotional outlook may be at the time.

TODAY

1. God can use even my depression for his glory.

2. I will seek ways to use my depression for God and not let depression use me.

3. I will make my own plan, using the suggestions from *Conquering Depression*, to overcome depression.